Access to History

General Editor: Keith Randell

Reaction and Revolutions: Russia 1881–1924

Michael Lynch

Hodder & Stoughton

LONDON SYDNEY AUCKLAND

The cover illustration shows Lenin (Courtesy Novosti Picture Library)

Other titles in the series:

Russia, Poland and the Ottoman Empire 1725–1800   ISBN 0 340 53334 X
Andrina Stiles
Russia, 1815–81   ISBN 0 340 54789 8
Russell Sherman
Stalin and Khrushchev: The USSR 1924–64   ISBN 0 340 52559 2
Michael Lynch
France in Revolution   ISBN 0 340 53494 X
Duncan Townson
The Unification of Germany, 1815–70   ISBN 0 340 51810 3
Andrina Stiles
The Unification of Italy, 1815–70   ISBN 0 340 51809 X
Andrina Stiles
**The Concert of Europe: International Relations
1815–70**   ISBN 0 7131 7828 0
John Lowe
Rivalry and Accord: International Relations 1870–1914   ISBN 0 340 51806 5
John Lowe

British Library Cataloguing in Publication Data
Lynch, Michael
    Reactions and revolutions: Russia 1881–1924.
    – (Access to history)
    I. Title   II. Series
    947.08

ISBN 0–340–53336–6

First published 1992
Second impression 1992

Typeset by Wearside Tradespools, Boldon, Tyne and Wear
Printed in Great Britain for the educational publishing division of Hodder & Stoughton Ltd, Mill Road, Dunton Green, Sevenoaks, Kent by Page Bros (Norwich) Ltd.

Contents

Preface

To the general reader

Although the *Access to History* series has been designed with the needs of students studying the subject at higher examination levels very much in mind, it also has a great deal to offer the general reader. The main body of the text (i.e. ignoring the Study Guides at the ends of chapters) forms a readable and yet stimulating survey of a coherent topic as studied by historians. However, each author's aim has not merely been to provide a clear explanation of what happened in the past (to interest and inform): it has also been assumed that most readers wish to be stimulated into thinking further about the topic and to form opinions of their own about the significance of the events that are described and discussed (to be challenged). Thus, although no prior knowledge of the topic is expected on the reader's part, she or he is treated as an intelligent and thinking person throughout. The author tends to share ideas and possibilities with the reader, rather than passing on numbers of so-called 'historical truths'.

To the student reader

There are many ways in which the series can be used by students studying History at a higher level. It will, therefore, be worthwhile thinking about your own study strategy before you start your work on this book. Obviously, your strategy will vary depending on the aim you have in mind, and the time for study that is available to you.

If, for example, you want to acquire a general overview of the topic in the shortest possible time, the following approach will probably be the most effective:

1. Read chapter 1 and think about its contents.
2. Read the 'Making notes' section at the end of chapter 2 and decide whether it is necessary for you to read this chapter.
3. If it is, read the chapter, stopping at each heading or * to note down the main points that have been made.
4. Repeat stage 2 (and stage 3 where appropriate) for all the other chapters.

If, however, your aim is to gain a thorough grasp of the topic, taking however much time is necessary to do so, you may benefit from carrying out the same procedure with each chapter, as follows:

1. Read the chapter as fast as you can, and preferably at one sitting.

2. Study the flow diagram at the end of the chapter, ensuring that you understand the general 'shape' of what you have just read.

3. Read the 'Making notes' section (and the 'Answering essay questions' section, if there is one) and decide what further work you need to do on the chapter. In particularly important sections of the book, this will involve reading the chapter a second time and stopping at each heading and * to think about (and to write a summary of) what you have just read.

4. Attempt the 'Source-based questions' section. It will sometimes be sufficient to think through your answers, but additional understanding will often be gained by forcing yourself to write them down.

When you have finished the main chapters of the book, study the 'Further Reading' section and decide what additional reading (if any) you will do on the topic.

This book has been designed to help make your studies both enjoyable and successful. If you can think of ways in which this could have been done more effectively, please write to tell me. In the meantime, I hope that you will gain greatly from your study of History.

Keith Randell

CHAPTER 1

Introduction

1 Outline of the Period, 1881–1924

In 1881 Russia was an empire, ruled over by an autocratic tsar. By 1924 it had become a Union of Soviet Socialist Republics, ruled over by a single political party. Such a remarkable transformation involved profound political, social and economic changes. This book attempts both to describe these and to explain why they occurred.

The period begins in 1881 with the adoption by the tsarist government of a policy of severe repression, which it maintained until 1905. The aim was the traditional one of crushing political opposition to the regime. Nevertheless, in 1905 a series of nationwide disturbances, which were serious enough to be referred to collectively as the 1905 Revolution, obliged the government to make some concessions. A duma (parliament) was introduced and became a feature of the political scene until 1917. However, the duma had not been intended by the tsar to be a genuine limitation on his autocratic powers. Between 1907 and 1914 its already restricted authority was increasingly eroded by further repression.

In spite of such government severity, a number of reforming and revolutionary parties had come into being by the first decade of the century. These represented a range of opinions, from the wish to see the tsarist system undergo moderate reform to the desire to see it swept away altogether. What had helped to stimulate both reformers and revolutionaries alike was a rapid period of industrial growth in the 1890s. This 'great spurt' seemed to offer a possibility that Russia might be able to throw off its backwardness. It is in this connection that one of the major historical controversies has arisen. There are those who contend that such was the rate of economic growth before 1914 that, had the First World War not intervened, Russia would have gone on to develop into a modern industrial society. Opposed to that line of argument are those who assert that the economic expansion was too superficial to sustain an industrial revolution on the scale required, and that in any case the tsarist political and social system was too reactionary and inflexible to be able to respond adequately to the demands of modernisation. They support their argument by claiming that the war which Russia entered in 1914 showed up the basic corruption and inadequacy of the tsarist system and made a major social and political upheaval unavoidable.

* Although the Russian Revolution in 1917 occurred near the end of the period in question, it is the centre-piece in terms of importance. According to some commentators, the years from 1881 to 1917 are best

See Preface for explanation of * symbol.

understood as a time of preparation for a revolution that had to come. Other observers suggest that this is to judge history with the advantage of hindsight and to adopt a 'determinist' approach – the assumption that, because something happened, it was necessarily and unavoidably caused by the events that preceded it. What gives edge to this particular historical debate is the Marxist interpretation of history. In the nineteenth century, Karl Marx, a German revolutionary, had advanced a theory which explained human history in terms of a set of inevitable class conflicts. The theory has proved highly influential. Marxist sympathisers continue to apply this analysis to the Russian situation. Their basic argument is that the Russian Revolution in 1917 was the essential first stage in the creation of a new state and society in which the workers ruled. Lenin, in accordance with Marxist strategy, had led the Bolshevik (Communist) Party to victory on behalf of the masses.

During the years following the 1917 Revolution, the Bolsheviks had to defend their revolution against the forces of reaction (generally referred to as the Whites) and to fight off attempted invasions of Soviet Russia by the western capitalist powers. They were successful in this and by 1924 Lenin's Bolshevik Party had laid the basis for the development of the USSR as the world's first socialist state. Soviet Russia thus became the leader of – and the model for – all other nations and peoples who aspired to revolutionary change. Basic to this Marxist analysis of what happened between 1917 and 1924 is the view that the Russian Revolution marked the beginning of the worldwide rising of the proletariat (the exploited working class) against the bourgeoisie (the exploiting capitalist class).

Non-determinist historians do not accept that the Russian Revolution was inevitable. They tend to stress the small scale of the Bolshevik rising. They do not deny that it was highly significant, but they question whether it was truly a mass movement and point to the fact that the Bolshevik government could sustain itself in power only by adopting a policy of state terror. This was shown clearly by the violent dissolution in 1918 of the Constituent Assembly (a democratically-elected body), which Lenin feared might challenge Bolshevik authority. Political repression was the outstanding characteristic of subsequent Soviet rule. Critics of Bolshevism further emphasise its failure to achieve revolution outside Russia. Lenin believed that once revolution had taken place in Russia it would quickly spread across Europe, but he miscalculated. Despite the Bolsheviks' creation in 1919 of the Comintern (Communist International) to organise worldwide revolution, Soviet Russia, at the time of Lenin's death in 1924, was still the only revolutionary state in a hostile, capitalist, world.

The extent and significance of the alterations within Russia in the years between 1881 and 1924 have made the period a particularly controversial one. Why did Russia undergo such changes? Were they inevitable? What role did individuals play in the process? Could Russia have modernised its backward economic and social structure without undergoing revolution? Did the seizure of power in 1917 by a revolutionary Bolshevik Party mark the dawn of a new freedom for the Russian people, or did it simply replace one form of authoritarianism with another? In terms of its significance for the rest of the world, there is an even more important question. Was the Russian Revolution a model for all peoples seeking freedom and justice, or was it a fraudulent tyranny which led necessarily to misery and oppression? It is questions such as these and the conflicting answers offered to them by historians and analysts that have produced continuing and highly emotive controversy and debate.

2 Interpretations of the Russian Revolution

There are almost as many viewpoints on the Russian Revolution as there are books written about it, but the following paragraphs describe the major features in this historiography. It must be remembered that there have been so many important studies of the subject that the listing is of necessity a very selective one. Nevertheless, although it does not include all the theories that have been put forward about the Revolution, it does indicate what are considered to be the major interpretations and disputes.

i) The traditional Soviet view – based on the writings of Lenin, that the Russian Revolution was part of an inevitable scientific process and that it marked the seizure of power by the Russian masses, led by the Marxist-inspired Bolshevik Party, which then went on to create a workers' state.

ii) The non-Bolshevik socialist view – first put forward by Kerensky, another leading participant in the events of 1917, that the Revolution began as a genuinely democratic movement, but was then hijacked by the Bolsheviks, an unrepresentative and oppressive clique.

iii) The 'Optimist' view – favoured by Russian *émigrés* (those who fled abroad to escape the Revolution) and advanced by such historians as George Katkov, that imperial Russia was steadily transforming itself into a modern, democratic, industrial society until weakened by the 1914–17 war and subverted by the Bolsheviks, who were in the pay of the German government.

iv) The modernisation theory – notably argued by George Kennan, that Russia's undoubted economic growth before 1917 was not matched by a comparable political maturity and that, therefore, tsardom broke down under the strains of war, to be replaced by the dictatorial regime of Lenin and the Bolsheviks. Kennan was influential in shaping the official attitude of the United States towards the USSR during the Cold War period after 1945. Another important contribution to the modernisation debate is the work of Theodore Von Laue, who suggests that the centralised methods necessary for Russia to achieve the degree of industrialisation demanded in a modern, competitive world were incompatible with the development of a genuinely representative system of government. Hence revolution was unavoidable.

v) The theory of deepening revolution – associated particularly with the American analyst, Crane Brinton, which asserts that events in Russia conformed to the pattern underlying all modern revolutions: the overthrow of the existing system, followed by an initial phase of moderate revolution, superseded by extremism and terror.

vi) The pro-Bolshevik western view – first stated by William Chamberlin in the 1930s, that it was the mass support of the depressed industrial workers that provided the Bolsheviks with the means of achieving power. Chamberlin wrote the first major study in English of the Revolution. His work stands alongside that of a later historian, E. H. Carr, as a standard narrative and reference.

vii) The Soviet revisionist view – first put forward in the post-Stalinist years by the Russian historian, Edward Burdzhalov, which played down the role of the Bolsheviks in 1917 and maintained that the Revolution was the result of the spontaneous rising of the workers. Burdzhalov created controversy within the Soviet Union since his ideas were very much in line with the writings of Lev Trotsky, who, despite having been Lenin's colleague and a key figure in the October *coup*, was disgraced and denounced during the Stalinist years 1927–53.

viii) The post-*glasnost* Soviet view – developed during the years of the Gorbachev reforms of the late 1980s. It approaches Russian history in a more open-minded way and admits that mistakes were made by the Bolsheviks. A noted supporter of this interpretation has been Dmitri Volkogonov, whose analysis of Stalinism included the remarkable view for a Soviet historian that Stalin's tyranny was in part a product of the authoritarianism of Lenin and the Bolsheviks after 1917. Volkogonov paid tribute to the work of the western historians, Leonard Schapiro and Robert Conquest, both of whom had originally been sympathetic to Soviet Communism but whose subsequent researches led them to depict it as essentially oppressive.

ix) The theory of 'the Unfinished Revolution' – associated particularly with the ideas of those sympathetic to Trotsky, which argues that a genuine workers' revolution occurred in 1917, but was later betrayed by Lenin's successors. According to this school of thought, which is powerfully represented by such writers as Isaac Deutscher and Adam Ulam, the initial revolutionary enthusiasm of the workers was destroyed by the deadening rule of the bureaucratic and repressive Communist Party of the Soviet Union (CPSU).

x) The non-determinist view – associated with such writers as Richard Pipes. This emphasises the role of individuals in shaping the Revolution by arguing against the notion of inevitability. In 1990 Pipes expressed his basic view of the origins of the Revolution and its importance in these terms:

> 1 The Russian Revolution was made neither by the forces of nature nor by anonymous masses but by identifiable men pursuing their own advantage. Although it had spontaneous aspects, in the main it was result of deliberate action. As such it is very properly
> 5 subject to value judgement . . . For the dispute is not only over what has happened in the past but also over what may happen in the future.

Readers may well find it useful to refer back to this list of ten general interpretations as they study the rest of this book.

Making Notes on 'Introduction'

Your aim following the reading of this chapter should be to make certain that i) you have understood the principal features of Russian history in this period, and ii) you are aware of the key issues and arguments relating to it. Try to write brief answers to the following questions. This will reveal whether or not you have grasped the important points.

1. What were the main developments in Russian history in the period 1881–1924?
2. Why is it appropriate to refer to the Russian Revolution of 1917 as the 'centre-piece' of this period?
3. Over what issues has there been most disagreement among commentators on Russian history in this period?

Studying 'Reaction and Revolutions'

The Russian Revolution is one of the most influential happenings in modern world history and casts a long shadow over events both before and after it. It is difficult, therefore, when studying Russian history before 1917, not to be conscious of what it is leading towards. In one sense, this is very helpful since it concentrates the mind on the important issues and developments. In another sense, it presents a problem in that it tends to lead to the assumption that the significance of pre-1917 Russian history can be measured only by reference to the Revolution. This can create an historical imbalance. To avoid this, it is best to think of chapters 1–4 (describing and analysing the developments between 1881 and 1917) as dealing with a topic that is important in its own right. The causal connections between events before and after 1917 are introduced in chapters 5 and 6; it is soon enough to think of the Revolution then.

If you are using this book purely as a means of studying the 1917 Revolution, chapters 5 and 6 onwards should provide an adequate introduction and treatment, but, since the war played such a critical role in preparing Russia for revolution, it would be safer to take your study back at least to 1914.

Economic developments are of central importance in the history of all countries, but they have a particular significance in Russian history. It was the economic situation which prepared the ground for the Revolution in 1917 and it was economic needs that determined the character of the Bolshevik regime that replaced tsardom after 1917. The student wishing to gain a sure grasp of economic trends in this period is advised to pay special attention to chapters 2, 3 and 8. Chapter 2 also introduces the reader to the main features of tsarist Russia and would make useful reading even for those intending to begin their studies with the Revolution itself.

Examiners are becoming increasingly interested in the period of the Bolshevik consolidation of power. A great deal of controversy revolves round the question of whether the later tyranny of Stalinism was prefigured in the system already established by Lenin's government before 1924. Chapters 7 and 8 will introduce the main developments and arguments relating to this theme.

At all levels of historical study considerable attention is now being directed towards an understanding of historiography – the writing and interpretation of history. The period of Russian history covered by this book is an extremely rich area for historiographical analysis. Chapters 1 and 9, in particular, offer a number of helpful pointers towards this aspect of the study of history.

CHAPTER 2

Imperial Russia

1 Introduction

In appearance, Russia in 1881 was a great empire. It covered over eight million square miles, an area equivalent to two and a half times the size of the USA. At its widest points, from west to east, it stretched for 5000 miles; at its longest points, north to south, it measured 2000 miles. It covered a large part of two continents. European Russia extended eastward from the borders of Poland to the Urals mountain range. Asiatic Russia extended eastward from the Urals to the Pacific Ocean. The greater part of the population, which quadrupled from 40 million to 165 million between 1815 and 1914, was concentrated in European Russia. It was in that part of the empire that the major historical developments had occurred and it was there that Russia's principal cities, Moscow and St Petersburg, the capital, were situated.

The sheer size of the Russian Empire tended to give an impression of great strength. This was misleading. The population contained a wide variety of peoples of different race, language, religion and culture. The difficulty of controlling and maintaining such a disparate number of peoples over such a vast territory had long been a major problem for Russian governments.

The major nationalities of the Russian Empire according to the census of 1897 (in millions, defined according to mother tongue)

Great Russian	55.6	Lithuanian	1.2
Ukrainian	22.4	Armenian	1.2
Polish	7.9	Romanian/Moldavian	1.1
White Russian	5.8	Estonian	1.0
Jewish (defined by faith)	5.0	Mordvinian	1.0
Kirgiz/Kaisats	4.0	Georgian	0.8
Tartar	3.4	Tadzhik	0.3
Finnish	3.1	Turkmenian	0.3
German	1.8	Greek	0.2
Latvian	1.4	Bulgarian	0.2
Bashkir	1.3		

2 The Tsarist Government

The peoples of the Russian Empire were governed by one person, the tsar (emperor). Since 1613 the Russian tsars had been members of the Romanov dynasty. By law and tradition, the tsar was the absolute ruler. Article I of the 'Fundamental Laws of the Empire', issued by Nicholas I in 1832, declared:

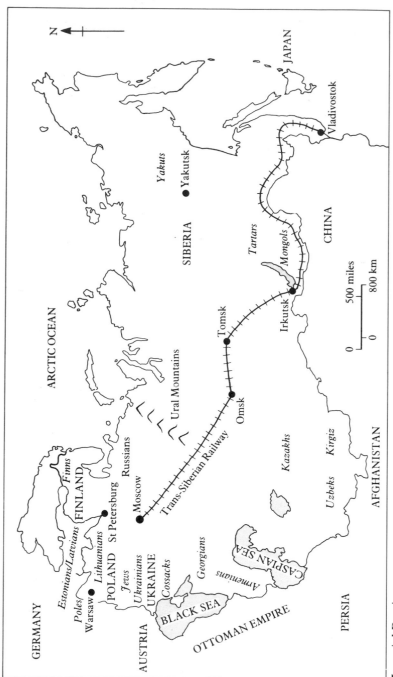

Imperial Russia

The Emperor of all the Russias is an autocratic and unlimited monarch; God himself ordains that all must bow to his supreme power, not only out of fear but also out of conscience.

There were three official bodies through which the tsar exercised his authority: the Imperial Council – a group of honorary advisers directly responsible to the tsar; the Cabinet of Ministers – concerned with the running of the various government departments; and the Senate – concerned with supervising the operation of the law. These bodies were much less powerful than their titles suggest. They were appointed, not elected, and their role was wholly advisory or administrative. In no way did they restrict the power of the tsar, whose word was the final authority in all matters of state and of law.

That the notion of an absolute, divinely-appointed monarch still prevailed in Russia in the late nineteenth century is a clear indication of how politically backward the country was in relation to the other major powers of Europe. It is true that many other states were monarchies (for example, Germany, Britain and Austria–Hungary), but in each of them there had been significant moves towards parliamentary or representative government. Although she had been frequently and closely involved in European diplomatic and military affairs, Russia had remained outside the mainstream of European political thought. Progressive tsars such as Peter I (1683–1725), Catherine II (1762–96) and Alexander II (1855–81) had taken bold steps to modernise the country, but their reforms had not included the extension of political rights or freedoms. In Russia in 1881 it was still a criminal offence to oppose the tsar or his government. There was no parliament, and political parties were not officially tolerated. State censorship was imposed on the press and on published books. Although this did not prevent liberal ideas from seeping into Russia, it did mean that they could not be openly advocated. The result was that supporters of reform or change had to go underground. In the nineteenth century there had grown up in Russia a wide variety of secret societies dedicated to political reform or revolution. But these groups were frequently infiltrated by agents of the *Okhrana*, the tsar's secret police. As a result, raids, arrests, imprisonment and general harassment were regular occurrences.

* Among Russia's governing classes there was a deeply ingrained prejudice against granting rights to the mass of the people. Over four-fifths of the population were peasants. They were predominantly illiterate and uneducated. Their sheer size as a social class and their uncivilised ways led to their being regarded with a mixture of fear and contempt by the small, educated, governing elite. The idea of the fundamental irresponsibility of the 'dark masses' who could be held in check only by severe repression was expressed by Alexandra, the wife of the last tsar, Nicholas II (1894–1917): 'Russia needs and loves the feel of the whip.' The denial of free expression tended to drive political activists towards extremism. The outstanding example of this was the assassination of Tsar Alexander II in 1881 by a terrorist group known as 'The People's Will' (see page 37). In a society in which state oppression vied with revolutionary terrorism, moderate opinion could make little headway. There was no middle ground on which a tradition of ordered political debate could develop.

3 The Russian Orthodox Church

The tsars were fully supported in their claims to autocracy by one of the great pillars of the Russian system, the Orthodox Church. This was a branch of Christianity which since the fifteenth century had been entirely independent of any outside authority such as the papacy. Its detachment from foreign influence had given it an essentially Russian character. The beauty of its liturgy and music had long been an outstanding expression of Russian culture. However, by the late nineteenth century it had become an essentially conservative body, opposed to political change and wholly committed to the preservation of the tsarist system in its reactionary form. The Church did contain some priests who strongly sympathised with the political revolutionaries, but as an institution it used its spiritual authority to teach the Russian people that it was their duty to be totally obedient to the tsar as God's anointed. The catechism of the Church (the primer used for instructing the people in the essential points of the faith) included the statement that 'God commands us to love and obey from the inmost recesses of our heart every authority, and particularly the tsar'.

4 The Social and Economic Structure of Tsarist Russia

a) Social Classes

An impression of the social structure of Russia in the nineteenth century can be gained from the following figures from the 1897 census, showing the distribution of the population, defined by class.

Ruling class (tsar, court, and government)	0.5%
Upper class (nobility, higher clergy, military officers)	12.0%
Commercial class (merchants, factory owners, financiers)	1.5%
Working class (factory workers and small traders)	4.0%
Peasants (land dwellers and agricultural workers)	82.0%

The outstanding features of this structure were the comparatively small commercial, professional and working classes and the huge preponderance of peasants in the population. Until 1861, half of the peasantry had only serf status; that is to say, they were the legal property of the landowners who made up the Russian nobility. The other half of the peasantry were only marginally freer than the serfs. They were

The Russian caption for each layer of the pyramid means, in descending order: *We rule you!*; *We persecute you!*; *We shoot you!* and *We exploit you!*

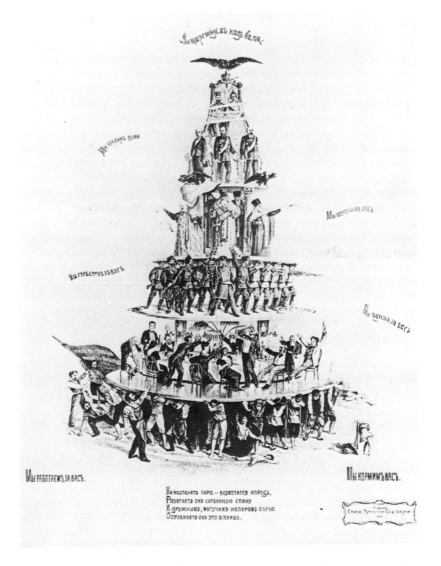

The social pyramid in imperial Russia – a socialist cartoon of 1900

referred to as state peasants, a term which indicated that, although they were not the possession of an individual landowner, they were technically the property of the state and were, therefore, subject to the authority of government agents and officials in the countryside. In 1861, in an attempt to produce greater stability and security in the rural areas, Tsar Alexander II had issued an Emancipation Decree abolishing serfdom.

b) Industry

The striking disproportion between the size of the urban professional and working classes and that of the rural peasants illustrated a critical aspect of imperial Russia; namely, her lack of economic development. The low numbers of urban workers indicated that Russia had not experienced the major industrial expansion that had occurred in the nineteenth century in such countries as Germany, Britain and the USA. This is not to say that Russia was entirely without industry. The Urals region produced considerable amounts of iron and the chief western cities, Moscow and St Petersburg, had extensive textile factories. Most villages had a smelting-works, and most peasant homes engaged in some form of cottage-industry, producing wooden, flaxen or woollen goods to supplement their income from farming. However, these activities were all relatively small-scale. The sheer size of Russia and her undeveloped system of roads and railways had proved an important limitation on industrial growth. An additional restriction had been the absence of an effective banking system. Russia did not have access to the readily-available capital for investment in industry that had stimulated developments in other countries. These factors had discouraged the rise of an entrepreneurial spirit, that dynamic, expansionist attitude that characterised western capitalism in this period.

c) Agriculture and the Peasantry

The lack of industrial enterprise in Russia was not compensated for by an efficient, productive system of agriculture. Even though four-fifths of the population were peasants, a thriving agrarian economy had not arisen. Indeed, the land in Russia was a source of national weakness rather than strength. The empire's vast acres were not all good farming country. Much of Russia lay too far north to enjoy a climate or a soil conducive to crop-growing or cattle-grazing. Land suitable for arable farming was restricted mainly to the Black Earth region, the area of European Russia stretching from the Ukraine in the west to Kazakhstan in the east. In addition, the size of the peasant population created its own problems. There was simply not enough land to go round. The peasants were entitled to buy land under the terms of the Emancipation Decree of 1861, but they invariably found its price excessively high.

This was caused both by a scarcity of suitable farming territory and by the government's taxation of property sales, imposed in order to raise the revenue needed to compensate the landowners for the losses caused by emancipation. The only way the peasants could raise the money to buy land was by borrowing from a special fund provided by the government. Consequently, those peasants who did manage to purchase property found themselves burdened with large mortgage repayments which would take them and their families generations to repay.

The high cost of land meant that few peasant families could afford to buy more than a few acres. The small areas that were purchased were normally subdivided into narrow strips in an attempt to provide each household within the family with some property, no matter how little. The result was greater inefficiency. The strip system, involving the use of antiquated farming implements and techniques, had long ago been abandoned in the agriculturally advanced nations. Its continuation in Russia was a major cause of her relative incapacity as a food-producing nation.

The existence in the second half of the nineteenth century of a largely illiterate peasantry, deeply conservative and resistant to change, and for the most part living in conditions of extreme poverty, was a testament to the social, political and economic backwardness of imperial Russia. Various attempts to educate the peasants had been made in the past, but such efforts had been undermined by the fear among the ruling class that any improvement in the conditions of the 'dark masses' might threaten its own privileges. It was commonplace for officials in Russia to speak of the 'safe ignorance' of the uneducated population, implying that any attempt to raise the educational standards of the masses would prove both socially and politically dangerous.

5 The Army

One method of keeping the peasant masses in check was to conscript numbers of them into the Russian armed services. The lower ranks of the army and navy were largely filled by enforced enlistment. As well as maintaining recruitment, conscription was frequently used as a form of punishment for law-breakers. The dread of conscription among ordinary Russians derived from their awareness that life in the army was invariably a brutalising experience. The Russian army was notorious in Europe for the severity of its discipline and the grimness of the conditions in which its soldiers lived. Special military camps had been set up in the remoter, more inhospitable regions of the empire which operated as penal colonies rather than as training establishments. It has been calculated that the rigours of service life had accounted for the deaths of over one million soldiers in peacetime during the reign of Nicholas I (1825–55). Throughout the nineteenth century the imperial Russian army maintained a strength of around one and a half million troops. The cost of maintaining the army and the navy accounted on average for 45 per cent of the government's annual expenditure. This was by far the largest single item and, when compared with the four per cent devoted to education, shows the order of priorities set by the government. It was a persistent Russian belief that, as a large empire, Russia required a large army.

*The structure of the armed services reflected the social imbalance within Russia as a whole. The higher ranks were the preserve of the aristocracy, who regarded the services as a legitimate area for the exercise of their privileges. Commissions were bought and sold, a symptom of the widespread corruption which underlay the organisation and maintenance of the Russian army. This necessarily made it less effective as a fighting force, but this fact tended to remain hidden because, with the exception of the Crimean War (1854–6), Russia was not engaged in a war with a western European power for a whole century after 1815. This meant that the army's active service was essentially a matter of putting down national risings or serious disturbances within the empire or on its frontiers. There were also frequent border wars with Turkey throughout the nineteenth century, and at various times Russian forces saw action in Poland, Armenia and Persia.

6 The Bureaucracy

Ironically, it was in the area where there had been the largest attempted reform that the greatest corruption had developed. Peter the Great had striven to modernise Russia by establishing a full-scale civil service as a means of exercising effective central-government authority throughout the empire. However, by the middle of the nineteenth century many critics within Russia had begun to assert that this civil service had become a corrupt bureaucracy whose nepotism, irresponsibility and incompetence were the principal reasons for Russia's backwardness. Alexander Herzen, a leading revolutionary writer, made the following charge in 1868:

> 1 One of the saddest consequences of Peter's revolution was the development of the official class. An artificial, hungry, and uneducated class, capable of doing nothing but 'serving', knowing nothing apart from official forms, it is a kind of civilian
> 5 priesthood, celebrating divine service in the law-courts and the police forces, and sucking the blood of the people with thousands of greedy, unclean mouths. There, somewhere in sooty offices which we hurry through, shabby men write page after page on grey paper, and make copies on embossed paper – and persons,
> 10 families, entire villages are outraged, terrified, ruined. A father is sent to exile, a mother to prison, a son to the army – and all this breaks over their heads like thunder, unexpected and usually undeserved.

Herzen's analysis is particularly instructive. Peter the Great's plan to westernise Russia had resulted in the creation of a bureaucratic class which, while incompetent and unenlightened, possessed the power to control the lives of the Russian people. At local and national levels the functioning of the law, civil administration, the police and the militia was in the hands of a set of officials whose first thought was its own convenience and advantage. Against this injustice the ordinary citizen had no redress, since any challenge to the system was lost in bureaucratic procedures.

Herzen's savage attack on the system provided powerful ammunition for those in Russia who wished to ridicule and undermine the apparatus of tsarist government. However, it is important to remember that Herzen was a revolutionary propagandist and was trying to paint the blackest picture he could of this aspect of tsardom. There is evidence from other sources which indicates that efforts were made in the nineteenth century to reform the administration, to limit its abuses, and to widen its social composition. Nonetheless, as so many of the novelists and political commentators, foreign as well as Russian, were at pains to show, the corrupt civil administration remained an outstanding scandal that did much to weaken the prestige and lower the morale of imperial Russia.

7 Reform

Many members of the ruling class accepted that major reforms were needed if Russia were to overcome her social and economic backwardness. However, a major block in the way of reform was a basic disagreement among the government elite concerning Russia's true character as a nation. Since the days of Peter the Great there had been serious differences within the government between 'Westerners' and 'Slavophiles'. The 'Westerners' believed it was essential for national greatness for Russia to see herself as essentially European and to adopt the best features of the political and economic systems of the advanced countries of western Europe. The 'Slavophiles' regarded western values with suspicion and urged that Russia should glory in and maintain her unique, separate, historical tradition.

Another barrier to planned reform was that, given the autocratic structure of Russian government with its absence of representative institutions, the only possible source of change was the tsar himself. From time to time there were progressive tsars who accepted the need for reform, but it was hardly to be expected that any tsar, no matter how enlightened, would go so far as to introduce measures that might weaken his authority. The tendency was, therefore, for reform to be sporadic, depending on the inclinations of individual tsars, rather than a systematic programme of modernisation. It is notable that the significant periods of reform in Russia were invariably a response to some form of national trauma or humiliation. This was certainly true of the reforms introduced in Alexander II's reign (1855–81). His coming to the throne coincided with the defeat of Russia at the hands of France and Britain in the Crimean War. The shock of this reverse prompted Alexander into a series of major changes in Russian society.

*These changes began with the emancipation of the serfs in 1861, followed three years later by the introduction of the *zemstva*, a network of rural councils set up with the aim of providing more efficient local government. Although the *zemstva* were elected bodies, they are not to be thought of as genuinely democratic, since the voting regulations left them very much in the hands of the landowners and local gentry. Nonetheless, they did provide Russia with a form of representative government, no matter how limited or localised, which offered some hope to those progressives who longed for an extension of political rights. The authorities complemented their introduction of the *zemstva* by re-emphasising the valuable role played in the countryside by the traditional *mir* (the village commune). Government officials saw in the *mir* a local organisation which would provide a relatively cheap means of collecting taxes and mortgage repayments and an effective way of maintaining order. In addition, a number of legal reforms were introduced, whose purpose was to streamline the cumbersome and protracted law-court procedures that had become a scandal of corruption and injustice.

Of even greater importance was Alexander II's relaxation of the controls over the press and the universities. Greater freedom of expression encouraged the development of a Russian 'intelligentsia'. This is best defined not as a single class, but as a cross-section of the educated and more enlightened members of society. Alexander was not a supporter of reform simply for its own sake. He saw it as a means of undermining opposition to the tsarist system. Before embarking on his policy of progressive changes, he had said that his intention was to introduce reform from above in order to prevent revolution from below. His hope was that his reforms would attract the new intelligentsia to the side of tsardom as natural allies. The early signs were that he had succeeded. The measures of the 1860s were greeted with enthusiasm by the intelligentsia, who believed that they might well form the basis of a genuine restructuring of Russian politics and society. However, regardless of how progressive Alexander II may have appeared to be, he was still an autocrat. It was unthinkable that he would continue with a process that might compromise his power as tsar. Fearful that he had gone too far, he had largely abandoned his reformist policies by the 1870s. Many of the intelligentsia felt betrayed. Despairing of tsardom as a force for change, a significant number of them turned to thoughts of revolution.

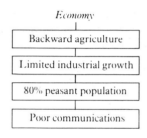

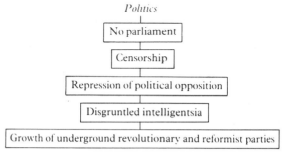

Summary – Imperial Russia

Making notes on 'Imperial Russia'

The objective of this chapter is to describe the basic features of imperial Russia. Read through each section and briefly list the key points. Remember that in studying this 'background' chapter your aim should be to gain a broad rather than a detailed grasp of the main characteristics of tsarist Russia, so you should try not to write more than a few phrases under each heading.

The following list suggests the way in which your notes might be structured.

1.   Introduction
1.1   The geography of Russia
1.2   The nationalities that made up the Russian Empire
2.   The Tsarist Government
2.1   The tradition of tsarist authority
2.2   Through what bodies did the tsar exercise his authority?
2.3   Why had Russia failed to advance politically?
2.4   Who referred to whom as 'the dark masses'?
3.   The Russian Orthodox Church
3.1   In what ways did the Orthodox Church support tsarist authority?

CHAPTER 3

Development and Reform 1881–1914

1 'The Reaction'

The reign of Tsar Alexander III (1881–94) could hardly have begun in worse circumstances. The new tsar came to the throne prematurely after his father had been blown to pieces by a terrorist bomb. The assassination was the work of 'The People's Will', a group of disaffected members of the intelligentsia reacting against Alexander II's apparent abandonment of his earlier liberalising policies. The new tsar's response was predictable. He turned his back on reform altogether and instituted a series of repressive measures that collectively became known as 'the Reaction'. Five of the assassins were summarily tried and executed. This was immediately followed by the introduction in 1881 of a Statute of State Security, which greatly increased government powers. Special government-controlled courts were set up, which operated outside the existing legal system. Judges, magistrates and officials who were sympathetic towards liberal ideas were removed from office. The authority and powers of the *Okhrana*, were extended, and censorship of the press was tightened. At its introduction in 1881, the Statute was described as a temporary measure brought in to deal with an emergency, but in essentials it remained in place until 1917. Lenin described it as 'the *de facto* constitution of Russia'. Under its terms further repression was introduced. The University Statute of 1887 brought the universities under strict government control. The *Zemstva* Act of 1890 decreased the independence of the local councils and empowered government officials to interfere in their decision-making.

These restrictive measures were accompanied by a deliberate policy of 'Russification', which was an attempt by Alexander III's government to restrict the influence of the national minorities within the Russian Empire. Russian was declared to be the official first language, thereby extending the traditional policy of making it the form in which law and government were conducted throughout the empire. The effect of this was to give officials everywhere a vested interest in maintaining the dominance of Russian values at the expense of the other national cultures. Discrimination against non-Russians, which had previously been a hidden feature of Russian public life, became more open and vindictive in the 1890s. State interference in national forms of administration, education and religion became frequent and systematic. The nationalities that suffered most from the discrimination of these years were the Baltic Germans, the Poles, the Finns, the Armenians and the Ukrainians. With hindsight, the tsarist policy of Russification can be seen as peculiarly ill-judged. At a critical stage in its development, when cohesion and unity were needed as never before, Russia chose to

treat half of its population as inferiors or potential enemies.
* Particular victims of 'Russification' were the Jews. Anti-semitism
was deeply ingrained in tsarist Russia. Fierce persecutions of the Jews
had long been a feature of Russian history. These acts of savagery,
referred to as 'pogroms', were customarily encouraged by the government as a form of blood-letting. The Jews, the majority of whom lived
in distinct districts or 'ghettos', were convenient and easily identifiable
scapegoats who could be blamed for Russia's difficulties, thus diverting
attention from the government's own failings. During the reign of
Alexander III the number of pogroms increased markedly – an
indication of the government's real, if unofficial, encouragement of this
particular form of state terrorism. A group of ultra-conservative
Russian nationalists, known as the 'Black Hundreds', were notorious
for their attacks upon the Jews. Over 600 new measures were introduced, imposing severe social, political and economic restrictions on
the Jewish population.

The tsarist persecution of the Jews was politically crass. It immediately alienated the great mass of the five million Jews in the
Russian population, large numbers of whom fled in desperation to
western Europe and North America, carrying with them a deep hatred
of tsardom. Those who could not escape stayed to form a large,
embittered, and disaffected community within the empire. It was no
coincidence that the 1890s witnessed a large influx of Jews into the
various revolutionary movements in Russia. In 1897, Jews formed their
own revolutionary 'Bund' or union.

The person most closely associated with the anti-semitic policies of
this period was Pobedonostsev, chief minister in the Russian government from 1881 to 1905 and director general of the Synod, the
governing body of the Russian Orthodox Church. An arch-conservative
by instinct and upbringing, he developed a deep distaste for all forms of
liberalism and democracy. He dismissed the idea of representative
government as 'the great lie of our time'. To his mind autocracy was the
only possible government for imperial Russia. As personal tutor to
Alexander III and Nicholas II, he played a major part in shaping the
essentially reactionary and illiberal attitudes of the last two tsars.
Known as 'the Grand Inquisitor' because of his repressive policies,
Pobedonostsev personified the obstructions in the way of Russia's
necessary political and social reform. One of the ironies of the Russian
history of this period was that 'the Reaction', associated with Alexander
III and Pobedonostsev, coincided with a time of remarkable economic
expansion. It is this fact that gives added weight to the argument that in
the late nineteenth and early twentieth centuries the tsarist government
threw away its last chance of survival. At a critical phase, when
economic developments seemed to offer a chance for Russia to modernise herself, tsardom showed a fatal resistance to change.

2 Witte and Economic Reform

In the 1890s, in marked contrast to the political repression of the time, Russia experienced industrial expansion on a scale that has attracted such descriptions as the 'great spurt'. A major contributory factor in this striking development was the rapid increase in the output of the coal in the Ukraine and of oil in the Caucasus. Economic historians are agreed that, although this sudden acceleration was initiated by private enterprise, it was sustained by deliberate government policy. The tsarist government's motives were military rather than economic. It is true that the capitalists (financiers and factory owners) did well out of the take-off, but it was not the government's intention to create a new capitalist class. The tsar and his ministers viewed industrialisation as a means of improving the military might of the Russian Empire.

The outstanding individual involved in this development was Sergei Witte, who, as minister of finance from 1893 to 1903, set himself the huge task of modernising the Russian economy to a level comparable with the advanced nations of the west. To help bring this about, he invited large numbers of foreign experts and workers to Russia to advise on industrial planning and techniques. Engineers and managers from France, Belgium, Britain, Germany and Sweden played a vital role in Russia's 'great spurt'. It was Witte's belief that modernisation could be achieved only through state capitalism – that is, through the effective use of state power to direct and control the economy. He was impressed by the results of the industrial revolutions in western Europe and the USA, and argued that Russia could modernise rapidly and effectively by planning along western lines. He admitted that, given the backwardness of Russia, this presented particular difficulties:

1 The economic relations of Russia to western Europe are fully comparable to the relations of colonial countries with their metropolises [mother countries]. The latter consider their colonies as advantageous markets in which they can freely sell the
5 products of their labour and of their industry, and from which they can draw with a powerful hand the raw materials necessary for them. Russia was, and to a certain extent still is, such a hospitable colony for all industrially developed states, generously providing them with the cheap products of her soil and buying
10 dearly the products of their labour. But there is a radical difference between Russia and a colony: Russia is an independent and strong power. She has the right and the strength not to want to be the handmaiden of states which are more developed economically.

* In Witte's judgement, Russia's outstanding need was for capital. He calculated that, without ready and sufficient supplies of finance,

Russia could not achieve the levels of investment required for genuine industrial expansion. In order to raise this capital and to put it to effective use, he adopted a number of interlocking policies. He negotiated large loans and investments from abroad, while imposing heavy taxes and high interest rates at home. At the same time as he encouraged the inflow of foreign capital, Witte limited the import of foreign goods. Protective tariffs were set up as a means of safeguarding Russia's young domestic industries. The decision was also made to put the rouble on the gold standard – making the rouble directly exchangeable for gold – thereby keeping Russian currency at a high value. This measure, together with the tariff policy, resulted in scarce goods and high costs within Russia.

Much of the foreign capital that Witte was successful in raising was directly invested in railways. It was his conviction that the expansion of the railway system was the essential basis on which the modernisation of the Russian economy depended. His enthusiastic support was a considerable factor in the extraordinary increase in lines and rolling stock that occurred between 1880 and 1914. It would not be an exaggeration to describe this as a transport revolution.

The growth of Russian railways (in kilometres)

1881	1891	1900	1913
21,228	31,219	53,234	70,156

Witte's special prestige project was the Trans-Siberian Railway, which was constructed between 1891 and 1902. The line stretched for over 6000 kilometres from Moscow to Vladivostok and was intended to open up the remoter regions of the central and eastern empire by connecting them with the industrial west, thereby encouraging the internal migration of workers and increasing Russia's production and export potential. However, it promised more than it delivered. Sections of it were still incomplete in 1914 and it did not greatly improve or increase east–west communications. On balance, the Trans-Siberian Railway proved more impressive as a symbol of Russian enterprise than as a project of real economic value.

One of Witte's main hopes was that the dramatic improvement in transport would stimulate the economy in such a way as to boost exports and foreign trade. The trade figures suggest a large measure of success in this regard.

The Russian balance of trade (in millions of roubles)

	Imports	Exports	Balance
1871–80	488	454	−34
1881–90	472	622	+150
1891–1900	535	660	+125
1901–10	887	1,073	+186

(In pre-1914 Russia the rouble was worth approximately 10p.)

The Russian economy: annual production (in millions of tons)

	Coal	Pig iron	Oil	Grain*
1880	3.2	0.42	0.5	34
1890	5.9	0.89	3.9	36
1900	16.1	2.66	10.2	56
1910	26.8	2.99	9.4	74
1913	35.4	4.12	9.1	90
1916	33.8	3.72	9.7	64

(*European Russia only)

Industrial output in the Russian Empire (base unit of 100 in 1900)

1900: 100	1909: 122.5
1904: 109.5	1911: 149.7
1905: 98.2	1912: 153.2
1906: 111.7	1913: 163.6

Some commentators have suggested that these figures of increased production are less impressive when it is remembered that Russia was experiencing a massive growth in population. Production per head of population was less striking than the aggregate figures.

Population of imperial Russia 1885–1913

	1885	1897	1913
European Russia	81,725,200	93,442,900	121,780,000
Caucasus	7,284,500	9,289,400	12,717,200
Siberia	4,313,700	5,758,800	9,894,500
Steppes and Urals	1,588,500	2,465,700	3,929,500
Central Asia	3,738,600	5,281,000	7,106,000
Russia (excluding Poland and Finland)	98,650,500	116,237,800	155,422,200

Growth of population in Russia's two main cities

	St Petersburg	Moscow
1881	928,000	753,500
1890	1,033,600	1,038,600
1897	1,264,700	1,174,000
1900	1,439,600	1,345,000
1910	1,905,600	1,617,700
1914	2,217,500	1,762,700

The scale of the problem Russia faced in attempting to overcome her economic backwardness is illustrated by a comparison of her growth rate and her foreign trade returns with those of the industrialised nations of the west:

Comparative growth in national income 1894–1913

Italy	121%	Austria	79%	Britain	70%
Germany	58%	France	52%	European Russia	50%

Foreign trade in 1913 (valued in £millions)

Russia	190	Austria-Hungary	199	France	424
		Germany	1030	Britain	1223

* There is no question that Witte's policics had a major effect on the growth of the Russian economy, but doubts have been expressed about whether that effect was wholly beneficial. Critics of Witte as an economic strategist have argued that he made Russia too dependent on foreign loans and investments, that in giving priority to heavy industry he neglected vital areas such as light engineering, and that he paid no attention to Russia's agricultural needs.

However, any criticism of Witte should be balanced by reference to the problems he faced. The inertia and resistance to change which characterised the court and the government severely restricted his freedom of action. In addition, military requirements often interfered with his plans for railway construction and the siting of industry. The main purpose of his economic policies was to protect tsardom against the disruptive elements in Russian society, but ironically he was distrusted by the royal court. Witte was faced with the dilemma that confronted any minister who sought to modernise tsarist Russia; he was regarded with suspicion by the representatives of the very system he was trying to save.

* The improvement of the Russian economy in the 1890s was not simply the result of the work of Witte. It was part of a worldwide industrial boom. However, by the turn of the century the boom had

ended and a serious international trade recession had set in. The consequences for Russia were especially serious. The industrial spurt of the last two decades of the century had led to a very rapid increase of population in the towns and cities. This increase had not been organised or supervised; the resources and facilities for accommodating the influx of workers were wholly inadequate. The result was acute overcrowding. Initially, the peasants who had left the land to take work in the urban factories accepted their grim conditions because of the considerably higher wages they were receiving. But when boom turned to recession there was widespread unemployment. The authorities in the towns and cities found themselves facing large numbers of rootless and disaffected workers who had had their expectations of a better life raised, only to be dashed by harsh economic realities. The regular presence on the streets of St Petersburg and Moscow of thousands of unemployed and embittered workers played an important part in the growth of serious social unrest in Russia between 1900 and 1917.

* The recession did not prove permanent. The period from 1908 to 1914 was one of overall recovery for the Russian economy, as the following figures indicate:

	1908	1914
State revenues	2 billion roubles	4 billion roubles
Number of banks	1146	2393
Number of factories	22,600	24,900
Number of workers	2.5 million	2.9 million

(Overall industrial growth-rate between 1908 and 1914 – 8.5%)

Against the bright picture presented by these figures has to be set the darker aspect. In general terms the industrial workers did not gain from the industrial and financial expansion. The absence of effective trade unions and the lack of adequate legal protection left the workforce very much at the mercy of the employers. Little of the greater amount of money in circulation reached the pockets of the workers. Although the rate of inflation rose by 40 per cent between 1908 and 1914, the average industrial wage rose from 245 to only 264 roubles per month in the same period. Of course, a national average does not tell the whole story. Some workers did relatively better than others – for example, in St Petersburg, wages were a third higher than in Moscow. Nonetheless, the strike statistics compiled by the Ministry of Trade showed the scale of the industrial unrest.

Number of strikes

1905	13,995
1908	892
1910	222
1911	466
1912	2,032
1913	2,404
1914	3,574

* The question of how strong the Russian economy actually was in 1914 remains a matter of lively debate among historians. There are those who suggest that until the war came Russia was in the process of developing into a modern industrial state. They cite figures showing increased industrial production, growth of the labour force, and expansion of foreign investment. Other historians, while accepting these figures, argue that, relative to developments in other countries, the Russian growth was too limited to provide a genuine industrial base. They further stress that in 1914 about four-fifths of the population were still peasants, a fact which would seem to discredit any claim that there had been significant industrial development. What complicates the debate is that political judgements often intrude. For example, Marxist sympathisers have tended to paint as black a picture as possible of the tsarist economy in order both to explain why revolution came and to emphasise the later achievements of the Russian Revolution in the economic sphere.

In the end, no definitive answer can be given to the question as to how the economy would have developed had the war and the Revolution not intervened. The comment of Alex Nove, the outstanding western authority on the Russian economy, is particularly telling:

1 The question of whether Russia would have become a modern industrial state but for the war and the revolution is in essence a meaningless one. One may say that statistically the answer is in the affirmative. If the growth rates characteristic of the period
5 1890–1913 for industry and agriculture were simply projected over the succeeding 50 years, no doubt citizens would be leading a reasonable existence ... However, this assumes ... that the imperial authorities would have successfully made the adjustment necessary to govern in an orderly manner a rapidly developing
10 and changing society ... But there must surely be a limit to the game of what-might-have-been.

3 Stolypin and Land Reform

Peter Stolypin was appointed president of the Council of Ministers in the aftermath of the 1905 Revolution (see page 45). Like Witte before him, he was dedicated to strengthening tsardom in a time of crisis. He was a political conservative, whose anti-liberalism was clearly expressed in his fierce suppression of opposition between 1906 and 1911. His statement, 'suppression first and then, and only then, reform', expressed his basic attitude. However, he judged that, where possible, reform should be introduced as a way of lessening the social bitterness that produced opposition. It was in this spirit that he approached the agrarian problem in Russia. It is helpful to regard the work of Witte and Stolypin as complementary, Witte being mainly concerned with the development of industry in Russia, Stolypin with the development of agriculture. This is not to suggest that the two men co-operated in a common policy. Indeed, they differed on a range of political and social issues. Nevertheless, they did share a basic objective – the preservation of the tsarist system. Indeed, it is sometimes suggested that the reforms they introduced represented the last hope that tsardom could save itself by its own efforts. Had the tsarist government and bureaucracy been willing to support Witte and Stolypin in their efforts to modernise the Russian economy, this might have prevented the build-up of the social and political tensions which culminated in the 1917 Revolution.

Stolypin appreciated that industrial progress could not of itself solve Russia's most pressing need – how to feed the nation's rapidly growing population. The peasants were the essential problem. Their grievances and sense of insecurity both inhibited them from being efficient food-producers and made them a dangerous social force, as illustrated by their involvement in the 1905 Revolution. The government's land policies following the emancipation of the serfs in 1861 had made the lot of the peasants worse rather than better. The scheme whereby state mortgages were advanced to the emancipated serfs to enable them to buy land had not created the system of stable land tenure that the government had anticipated. The high price of land, which led to heavy mortgage repayments being undertaken, had impoverished the peasantry. The population explosion that occurred in the late nineteenth century had added to the problem by creating land shortage and rural over-population. A series of bad harvests had further increased the woes of rural Russia. One of the reasons why the peasants had joined the Revolution in 1905 was their fear that the government was about to repossess the land of the mortgage-holders who had defaulted on their payments. When the government came to understand this fear, it bought off the peasants by announcing that the outstanding repayments would be cancelled.

Stolypin planned to build upon this successful 'de-revolutionising' of the peasantry. In 1906 and 1907 he introduced measures which allowed the individual peasant to opt out of the commune-system. The authority of the *mir* was reduced and the idea of the independent householder was promoted. Peasants were encouraged to replace the antiquated strip system with consolidated farm-holdings, based on the pattern that existed in western Europe. A special Land Bank was established to allocate funds to assist the independent peasant to buy his land. Stolypin defined his policy as 'the wager on the strong'. His aim was to create a stratum of prosperous, efficient peasants whose new wealth would turn them into natural supporters and allies of the tsarist system. This would effectively decapitate the peasantry as a revolutionary movement. He complemented his land reform policy by supporting schemes already in existence for large-scale voluntary resettlement of the peasant population. The aim was to populate the empire's remoter areas, such as Siberia, and bring them into productive agricultural use.

* Even in advanced economies it is invariably the case that land reforms take time to work. Stolypin was well aware that, in a country as relatively backward as Russia, reforms would take even longer to become effective. He spoke of needing 20 years for his 'wager on the strong' to show dividends. In the event, his assassination in 1911 allowed him personally only five, and the war in 1914 allowed Russia only eight. However, there is doubt whether, even had he not been murdered and Russia had not entered the war, his peasant policy would have succeeded. The deep conservatism of the Russian peasants made them slow to respond. In 1914 the strip system still prevailed; only about 10 per cent of the land had been consolidated into farms. The peasants were reluctant to leave the security of the commune for the uncertainty of individual farming. Furthermore, by 1913 the Ministry of Agriculture had itself began to show signs of losing confidence in the feasibility of the policy.

Number of peasant households becoming independent
(out of an estimated total of 10–12 million households)

1907: 48,271	1908: 508,344	1909: 579,409	1910: 342,245
1911: 145,567	1912: 122,314	1913: 134,554	1914: 97,877

Stolypin was assisted in his land policy by his effective working relations with the duma. This elected assembly, which had been set up under the terms of the tsar's October Manifesto in 1905 (see page 48), had not been granted legislative rights. Nicholas II never intended the duma to be a direct limitation on his authority, and its powers were severely restricted. Nonetheless, it did provide for the first time in Russian history a forum for public discussion at national level. Stolypin chose to treat it with respect. The understanding which developed between between him and the Octobrists, the largest party in the duma, allowed him to pursue his land reforms with little obstruction from the duma deputies. His success in this regard hinted at what might have been achieved in terms of co-operation between government and the representatives of progressive opinion, had the tsarist authorities been willing to trust their own ministers.

4 Russian Foreign Policy

a) Russian Objectives

The foreign policy of tsarist Russia was largely determined by the size of her empire. The protection of her many frontiers was a constant preoccupation. There were three particular and connected developments which worried Russia with respect to her European borders: the growth of a united Germany, the formation of the Austro-Hungarian Empire, and the continued decline of the Turkish Empire. Russia feared that the unification of Germany in 1871 had left central Europe dominated by a young and powerful nation, ambitious to expand eastwards. Moreover, the process of German unification had involved the military and diplomatic defeat of Austria. Russia was concerned that the Austro-Hungarian Empire, which had been newly-formed in 1867, would try to repair its damaged prestige by an expansionist policy in south-east Europe. This might be made possible by the decay of Turkey's authority over its possessions in the Balkans, where numbers of aggressive national movements were challenging Turkish rule.

Russia's attitude towards Turkey was governed by two factors. One was her traditional wish, as a predominantly Slav nation, to protect the Slav Christian peoples of the Balkans from Turkish Islamic oppression. The other was an economic necessity. Of Russia's grain exports, 75 per cent (which accounted for 40 per cent of her total foreign trade) were shipped through the Straits of the Dardanelles. It was, therefore, necessary to ensure that the Straits did not come under the control of a potentially hostile power which would be able to interrupt the passage of Russian ships from the Black Sea into the Mediterranean.

* Russia's anxieties about the strength and intentions of the European powers led to her taking a basically cautious and conciliatory approach towards them. During the reigns of the last two tsars, Russia's response to the shifts and turns of European diplomacy was consistently self-protective and defensive. She was reluctant to take the diplomatic initiative, but she was willing to enter into alliances and agreements which offered a greater chance of preserving the security of her western borders and possessions. In particular, she was concerned that her traditional control over Poland should not be weakened. Things augured well for Russia at the beginning of Alexander III's reign. In response to a proposal of Bismarck, the German chancellor, Russia joined Austria-Hungary and Germany in the League of the Three Emperors (1881), an agreement by which each of the powers promised not to support the enemy should any of them become involved in war with a fourth country. This accord did not survive long. In the mid-1880s tension arose between Russia and Austria-Hungary over the latter's support for anti-Russian movements in Bulgaria. The Three Emperors League was not renewed. In its place, Russia and Germany signed a secret Reinsurance Treaty (1887), which recognised

Russian claims in Bulgaria and promised German neutrality in the event of a Russo-Austrian war.

b) Russia and the Alliance System

These diplomatic shifts testified to Bismarck's ability to dominate the European scene by playing upon the fears of each nation of becoming isolated in a world of alliances. However, in 1890 Bismarck was dismissed by the new German kaiser, William II. Under its new ruler, Germany adopted a more aggressive form of diplomacy which had the effect of polarising international attitudes, and led eventually to the splitting of Europe into two opposed, armed camps. William II declined to renew the Reinsurance Treaty. Instead, he showed every intention of joining with Austria in asserting German influence in the Balkans and the Near East. Russia feared isolation. She turned first to France, a country with whom her previous relations had been extremely hostile. A common fear of German belligerence now outweighed their traditional dislike of each other. The Franco-Russian Convention, signed in 1892 and confirmed in 1894, committed each partner to the military support of the other should it be at war with Germany. Their economic co-operation also brought them closer. France was the major foreign investor and supplier of loans to Russia during her industrial take-off in the 1880s and 1890s. The original alliance between France and Russia expanded into the Triple Entente, with the inclusion of Britain in 1907.

   * This, too, was something of a diplomatic revolution. Anglo-Russian relations had not been good for decades. Imperial rivalries in Asia and Britain's resistance to what it perceived as Russia's attempts to dominate the eastern Mediterranean had created a wide gulf between the two countries. Indeed, during the 1890s Britain seemed more drawn to the Triple Alliance than to France and Russia. However, by the turn of the century Germany had embarked on a major naval programme which Britain interpreted as a direct threat to the maintenance of her own security and to that of her empire. This, together with the kaiser's truculent anti-British stance, embittered Anglo-German relations. It was logical, therefore, that Britain should seek to balance the German threat by forming an understanding with Germany's major western and eastern neighbours, France and Russia. In the Anglo-French Entente of 1904, Britain and France had already agreed to abandon their old rivalry. It made diplomatic sense for Russia and Britain to do the same. Consequently, in 1907 they formally agreed to settle their past differences by recognising each other's legitimate interests in Afghanistan, Persia and Tibet. No precise agreement was reached regarding the matter of military co-operation in Europe, although the fact that Britain joined Russia and France in high-level military discussions created the general understanding that such co-

operation would follow in the event of war.

c) The Russo-Japanese War 1904–5

What had helped prepare the way for the Anglo-Russian *rapprochement* was the Russo-Japanese War of 1904–5. This struggle arose in part from Russia's decision to pursue an expansionist policy in the Far East, both as a means of compensating for her relative decline in Europe and as a way of obtaining an ice-free port. It was also an attempt by the tsarist government to distract attention from Russia's domestic troubles by rallying the nation in a patriotic struggle. Care has to be taken over this last point. Customarily, the blame for Russia's going to war against Japan has been laid upon Plehve, the minister of the interior. However, recent research has shown that this verdict rests upon misinformation deliberately spread by Witte. Richard Pipes observes:

1 The origins of the Russo-Japanese conflict have long been distorted by the self-serving accounts of Sergei Witte . . . Plehve's bitter enemy, which assigned the responsibility partly to reactionaries anxious to divert attention from internal difficulties ('We
5 need a small, victorious war to avert a revolution' was a sentiment he attributed to Plehve) . . . It has since become known that Plehve did not want a war . . . Witte himself bore a great deal of the blame for the conflict . . . Witte's plans for economic penetration of the Far East . . . called for a strong military presence,
10 which was sooner or later to come into conflict with the imperial ambitions of Japan.

Japan was judged by the Russians to be a semi-feudal state, and no match for themselves. Pretexts for war were not hard to find. Territorial disputes between Russia and Japan over Korea and Manchuria had simmered for some time. In 1904, the Russian authorities deliberately rejected Japanese proposals for the settlement of the Korean question in the hope that this would occasion a military response. The ruse worked: Japan opened hostilities by attacking the Russian fleet in Port Arthur. That proved to be the only accurate calculation made by the Russian government in the whole affair. The rest was a tale of confusion and disaster. Japan was not the backward state the Russians had imagined. Her army and navy were far better prepared and equipped than the Russian forces and they won a series of major victories. After a long siege, Port Arthur fell to Japan in January 1905. The following month, the Japanese forced home their advantage by driving the Russians out of the key Manchurian town of Mukden. The final catastrophe for Russia came at sea. The Russian Baltic fleet, dispatched to the Far East in 1904, took eight months to reach its destination, only to be blown out of the water immediately on its arrival by the Japanese fleet at Tsushima in May 1905. Such defeats obliged the tsarist government to make peace. Under the auspices of the United States, the Treaty of Portsmouth was signed between the belligerents. Russia agreed to withdraw her remaining forces from Manchuria and accepted Japanese control of Korea and Port Arthur.

Russia lost the war not because her troops fought badly, but because her military commanders had not prepared effectively. They understood neither the enemy they were fighting nor the territory in which the struggle took place. Their strategy was faulty and their tactics were unimaginative, which invariably allowed the Japanese to outmanoeuvre the Russian forces. The distance over which men and materials had to be transported from western Russia made it impossible for her to provide the necessary reinforcements and supplies. The Trans-Siberian Railway, still incomplete in a number of sections, proved of little value in this regard. Russia's comprehensive defeat at the hands of a small, supposedly inferior, Asian country was an undeniable humiliation, which mocked her claims to be a great imperial power. Within Russia, the incompetence of the government, which the war glaringly revealed, excited the social unrest which it had been specifically designed to dampen.

c) The Balkans

Russia's defeat in Asia had the important effect of redirecting her attention towards Europe and making her even keener to enter into protective alliances with friendly European powers. The area of most immediate concern was the Balkans. The revolt of the 'Young Turks' against the sultanate in 1908 marked a further stage in the collapse of Turkish power. Despite the wrangling that went on between their various ambassadors in the Balkan states, Russia and Austria-Hungary seemed genuinely willing to co-operate at government level. In 1908 at Buchlau, the Russian foreign minister, Izvolski, was urged by his Austro-Hungarian counterpart, Aehrenthal, to accept the annexation of Bosnia and Herzegovina by Austria-Hungary as a means of creating greater stability in the Balkan region. Izvolski agreed to the proposal in return for Austria-Hungary's promise that she would acknowledge Russia's unfettered right to the use of the Straits, and would persuade the other European powers to do the same. Austria-Hungary duly announced the takeover of Bosnia and Herzegovina, but, to the anger of Russia, made no attempt to initiate the international recognition of her rights in regard to the Straits.

* From this time onwards, relations between Russia and Austria-Hungary steadily deteriorated. A key issue dividing them was the position of Serbia. Bosnia contained many Serbs and its annexation by Austria-Hungary aroused fierce Serbian nationalism. Russia, viewing herself as the special defender of the predominantly Slav people of

Serbia, backed that country in demanding compensation and the convening of an international conference to consider the annexation. Germany sided aggressively with Austria-Hungary and issued what in effect was an ultimatum, demanding that Russia refrain from interfering. This crisis threatened for a time to spill into war. However, in 1909 none of the countries involved felt ready to fight. Russia backed off from an open confrontation, while at the same time letting it be known internationally that she regarded Germany and Austria-Hungary as aggressors.

Between 1909 and 1914 Russia continued to involve herself in the diplomatic complexities of Balkan nationalist politics. Her aim was to prevent Austria-Hungary from gaining a major advantage in the region. Her method was to try to persuade the various nationalities in the region to form a coalition against Austria-Hungary. She had some success in this. Balkan nationalism led to a series of conflicts, known collectively as the Balkan Wars (1912–13). These were a confused mixture of anti-Turkish uprisings and squabbles between the Balkan states themselves over the division of the territories they had won from the Turks. On balance, the outcome of these wars favoured Russian rather than Austro-Hungarian interests. Serbia had been strengthened and felt herself more closely tied to Russia as an ally and protector, while Austria-Hungary's client states, Romania and Bulgaria, had not not done well in the wars. However, such gains as Russia had made were marginal. The international issues relating to Turkish decline and Balkan nationalism, and the involvement of the European powers in them had not been resolved. The events of 1914 were to show how vulnerable Russia's status and security as a great empire actually were.

5 Conclusion

Between 1881 and 1914 Russia took a number of significant steps towards modernisation. Serious efforts were made to reform the economy; something approaching an industrial revolution took place, and progressive agricultural changes were introduced. Important adjustments were made in foreign policy in an effort to end old antagonisms and provide greater national security. These were not inconsiderable achievements. Foreign observers commented favourably on the advances that had been made. However, a fundamental question still remained unanswered in 1914. Was Russian capable or, indeed, willing to adopt the political and social changes necessary for her to become a modern nation? Although there had been some modifications of tsarist authority during the period, including the introduction of the duma, Russia in 1914 remained essentially an absolutist state. Reaction rather than reform had been the predominant theme. The willingness of the regime to preside over the transition of Russia from authoritarian to representative government seemed as remote in 1914 as in 1881.

Reaction	Reform	Foreign affairs
POBEDONOSTSEV (1881–1905)		Three Emperors League 1881
Statute of State Security 1881	WITTE (1893–1903)	
	'The great spurt'	German question
University Statute 1887	Population growth	
Zemstva Statute 1890	Foreign capital	Austro-Hungarian-Turkish Question
	Investment	
	Railways	
	Regional development	Franco-Russian Convention 1892
Russification	Industrial output	
Anti-Jewish Laws		
		Russo-Japanese
Pogroms	October Manifesto 1905	War 1904–5
The Black Hundreds	Dumas 1906–14	
	STOLYPIN (1906–11)	Triple Entente 1907
	Land reform	
The Stolypin repression 1906–11	Debt cancellation	
	Land bank	The Balkan crises 1908–14
	'Wager on the strong'	

Summary – Development and Reform 1881–1914

Making notes on 'Development and Reform 1881–1914'

The chapter takes a broadly chronological approach in its analysis of the principal features of government repression and reform during this period. You are advised to follow the same pattern when making your notes, which need to be quite detailed if you are studying this topic in its own right, rather than merely as a background to the Russian Revolution. The following headings and questions should help you to arrange your ideas in a convenient and readily accessible form.

1.   'The Reaction'
1.1. The terms of the Statute of State Security of 1881
1.2. What were the essential characteristics of 'Russification'?
1.3. The role of Pobedonostsev

2. Witte and Economic Reform
2.1. The reasons for the 'great spurt'
2.2. The connection between Witte's financial and industrial policies
2.3. What role did the railways play in Witte's plans?
2.4. The statistics of industrial growth
2.5. The debate on the character of Russian economic growth before 1914
3. Stolypin and Land Reform
3.1. How far did Stolypin and Witte follow a common policy?
3.2. Russian agriculture in the post-emancipation period
3.3. What do you understand by Stolypin's 'wager upon the strong'?
3.4. How successful had Stolypin's land reforms proved by 1914?
4. Russian Foreign Policy
4.1. The underlying objectives of tsarist foreign policy
4.2. The formation of the Triple Entente
4.3. Russian war aims in 1904
4.4. The results of the Russo-Japanese War
4.5. Russia's Balkan strategy before 1914
5. Conclusion
5.1. How far did imperial Russia modernise in the period 1881–1914?

Source-based questions on 'Development and Reform 1881–1914'

The economic reforms of Witte and Stolypin
Study Witte's analysis on page 21, the tables of statistics on pages 22 to 26, and then answer the following questions:
a) Using only the evidence in the source on page 21, explain the meaning of the following extract:
   'The economic relations of Russia to western Europe are fully comparable to the relations of colonial countries with their metropolises' (lines 1–3). (3 marks)
b) How far do the two tables on page 23, showing the balance of trade and annual production, suggest that Stolypin had achieved his economic objectives? (4 marks)
c) In the light of the tables on page 23 giving the figures of industrial output and of the population of imperial Russia, consider the statement that 'Production per head of population was less striking than the aggregate figures'. (5 marks)
d) Account for the fluctuations in the annual numbers of peasant households leaving the land between 1907 and 1914, as shown in the table on page 28. (5 marks)
e) How valuable are these sources to the historian who is involved in the debate over the real strength of the tsarist economy in 1914? (7 marks)

CHAPTER 4

Opposition to Tsardom 1881–1914

1 Introductory Survey

'The Reaction' that began under Alexander III and continued in the reign of Nicholas II (1894–1917) oppressed, but did not destroy, opposition to the tsarist regime. Indeed, despite greater police surveillance, opposition became more organised. A range of political parties, from the moderate reformist centre to the extreme revolutionary left, came into being. The rapidly-growing population, the economic acceleration and the government's policies of reaction and Russification, combined to produce a situation in which many political and national groups were becoming increasingly frustrated by the mixture of coercion and incompetence that characterised the tsarist system during this period. The rapid industrial growth in the 1890s brought to the cities large numbers of peasants, who were attracted by the prospect of relatively well-paid factory work. The subsequent depression in the first decade of the twentieth century left many of these new industrial workers unemployed, disillusioned and angry. As such, they were a serious threat to social order and stability.

The government attempted to meet the problem by diverting attention away from domestic issues with a war against Japan in the Far East. The aim was to unite the nation, but the reverse happened. Russia's humiliating military defeat in 1905 was blamed directly on the government's inept handling of the war. It was no coincidence that workers, peasants and middle-class liberals joined together in the year of Russia's defeat in a series of anti-government protests, which were serious enough to merit the description 'the 1905 Revolution'.

The disturbances obliged Nicholas II to make a number of political concessions. In his October Manifesto, he reluctantly gave in to the demand for the formation of a duma. That this was not a liberalising of the regime was illustrated by the ferocity of the political repression that followed after 1905. The government, led by Stolypin as chief minister from 1906 to 1911, was ruthless in its crushing of opposition. Notwithstanding the repression, strikes and disturbances continued. By 1914, many reformists had become so disillusioned with the failure of the 1905 Revolution to lead to real advance that they had begun to consider violence as the only means by which to change the oppressive yet incapable tsarist regime.

Until the issuing of the October Manifesto in 1905, political parties were illegal in Russia. This had not actually prevented their formation, but it had had the effect of making them necessarily conspiratorial organisations. Since this stifled their development as genuinely democratic bodies, they tended to resort to extreme methods in order to spread their ideas. As a result, during the brief period of their legal existence from 1905 to 1921, the Russian political parties proved generally to be highly suspicious and intolerant of each other. This made co-operation and collective action difficult to organise and sustain. Four main groups opposed to tsardom can be identified: the Populists, the Social Revolutionaries, the Social Democrats, and the liberals.

2 The Populists (*Narodniks*)

Populism dated from the 1870s. It was a revolutionary movement, which regarded the future of Russia as being in the hands of the peasants who made up the overwhelming mass of the population. The Populists or *Narodniks* (from the Russian word for 'the people') looked to the peasants to take the lead in the transforming of Russia, beginning with the overthrow of the tsarist system itself. As with all the significant political movements that came into being in this period, the Populist leaders were drawn, not from the peasants, but from the middle and upper classes. The Populists regarded it as their duty to educate the uninformed peasantry into an awareness of its revolutionary potential. This involved their 'going to the people', a policy by which the educated Populists went from the universities into the countryside to live for a period with the peasants in an attempt to incite them to revolution. The scheme met with little success. The peasants either did not understand or were unmoved by the revolutionary socialist message preached to them. In desperation, some Populists turned to terrorism, which they defined euphemistically as 'the propaganda of the deed', as the only way of achieving their aims. In 1879, a group calling itself 'The People's Will' was founded with the declared intention of murdering members of the ruling class. This group, which was reckoned to be no more than 400 strong, gained dramatic notoriety two years later with its assassination of Alexander II. However, this act weakened rather than strengthened the Populist movement. The murder of a tsar who had initiated many reforms seemed to discredit the idea of reform itself and so justified the repression imposed in the aftermath of the assassination.

The importance of Populism lay in its methods rather than in its ideas. Its concept of a peasant-based revolution appeared unrealistic, given the political ignorance and inertia of the Russian peasantry. What was lasting about Populism was the part it played in establishing a revolutionary tradition. All the revolutionaries of late nineteenth- and early twentieth-century Russia were influenced, if not inspired, by the example of the Populist challenge to tsardom.

3 The Social Revolutionaries (SRs)

The Social Revolutionary Party grew directly out of the Populist movement. The quickening of interest in political and social issues which accompanied the economic spurt of the 1890s was viewed by Populists as an opportunity to gain recruits for their revolutionary cause. They attempted to broaden their basis of appeal in order to attract the rapidly growing urban workforce to their traditionally peasant-orientated programme. The intention was to widen the concept of the 'people', so that it encompassed all those elements in society that had reason for wishing to see the destruction of the tsarist system. An important figure in this reshaping of Populist strategy was Victor Chernov, who played a major part in the formation of the Social Revolutionary Party in 1901 and became its leader. He was a member of the intelligentsia, and sought to provide a firmer theoretical base for Populism than its previous passionate but vague ideas had produced. However, as with all the revolutionary groups in tsarist Russia, the SRs were weakened by disagreements among themselves. Trotsky described them in these terms:

1 [They were] formed at the beginning of the century from a fusion
  of several tendencies of the *Narodniks*. Representing the wavering
  interests of the small peasant proprietor, the party soon split into
  a group of Left Social Revolutionaries, anarchist in their leanings,
5 and the Right Social Revolutionaries.

In distinguishing between the left and the right elements, Trotsky was referring to the division of the SR Party into anarchists and revolutionaries. The former were the faction who wanted to continue the policy of terrorism inherited from 'The People's Will'. The latter were the more moderate element, who, while believing in revolution as their ultimate goal, were prepared to co-operate with other parties in working for an immediate improvement in the conditions of the workers and peasants. Between 1901 and 1905, it was the terrorist faction that dominated. During those years the SRs were responsible for over 2000 political assassinations, including Plehve, the interior minister, and the tsar's uncle, the Grand Duke Sergei. These were spectacular successes but they did little to bring about the desired link with the urban workers.

The 1905 Revolution brought more gains to the liberals than to the revolutionaries (see page 48). One effect of this on the SRs was that the more moderate element gained greater influence over party policy. This began to show dividends. From 1906, the SR Party experienced a growing support from the professional classes, from the trade unions (which had been legalised under the October Manifesto), and from the All-Russian Union of Peasants, which had been set up in 1905. At its first congress in 1906, the SR Party committed itself to 'revolutionary socialism', and gave a special pledge to the peasants that it would end 'the bourgeois principle of private ownership by returning the land to those who worked it'. It was their land policy which largely explains why the SRs remained the most popular party with the peasants. However, at the time, the congress decisions brought disruption rather than unity. The left wing broke away on the grounds that the party's programme ignored the industrial proletariat, while the right wing complained that congress policy was unworkable in current Russian conditions. Chernov tried to hold the factions together, but from 1906 onwards the SRs constituted a collection of radical groups rather than a genuinely co-ordinated party.

4 The Social Democrats (the SDs)

The All-Russian Social Democratic Labour Party was formed in 1898. It was a Marxist party. That is to say, it accepted the theories of Karl Marx, the German revolutionary (1818–83). Marx had advanced the idea that the character of human society was determined by scientific laws which could be studied, understood, and then applied. His own understanding was that history was a continuous series of class struggles between those who possessed economic and political power and those who did not. The form of the conflict changed according to the historical period, but the essential struggle between the haves and the have-nots remained. This process of continuous class struggle was referred to as the dialectic. For revolutionaries in the nineteenth century, the most exciting aspect of Marx's historical analysis was his assertion that the contemporary industrial era marked the final stage of the dialectical class struggle. Human history was about to reach its culmination in the revolutionary victory of the proletariat (the industrial working class) over the the bourgeoisie (the exploiting, capitalist, class).

The attraction of Marx for Russian revolutionaries is easy to understand. His ideas had been known in Russia for some time, but what gave them particular relevance and appeal was the 'great spurt' of the 1890s. This promised to create the industrial conditions in Russia which would make a successful revolution possible. The previously loose and un-directed hopes for revolution could now be focused on the industrial working class. The first Marxist revolutionary of note in Russia was George Plekhanov. He had translated Marx's writings into Russian, and in 1883 had helped to found the first Marxist organisation in the country, the 'Group for the Emancipation of Labour'. His efforts to promote the idea of proletarian revolution had earned him the title 'the father of Russian Marxism'. Despite this, a number of the revolutionaries who had formed the SD Party in 1898 soon became impatient with Plekhanov's leadership. They found him too theoretical in his approach, and urged the adoption of more active revolutionary policies.

* The outstanding spokesman for this viewpoint was Vladimir

Ulyanov, better known by his revolutionary pseudonym as Lenin. Born in 1870 into a middle-class family, Lenin had been on the tsarist authorities' list of 'dangerous persons' since he was 17. The execution of his elder brother in 1887 for his part in an attempted assassination of Alexander III had made Lenin himself politically suspect. He lived up to his reputation. By the age of 20, his voracious reading of Marx's writings had turned him into a committed Marxist for whom revolution was a way of life. By the age of 30, his dedication to the cause of revolution in Russia had led to arrest, imprisonment, and exile. Indeed, he was in exile in Siberia when the SD Party was formed in 1898. When he returned to western Russia two years later he set about turning the SD into a genuinely revolutionary party. With an SD colleague, Julius Martov, he founded a party newspaper, *Iskra* (the Spark), which he used as the chief means of putting his case to the party members. Lenin was concerned that Plekhanov was more interested in reform than in revolution. He was worried that the SDs were attempting to improve the conditions of the workers (a policy referred to as 'economism'), instead of pursuing their true goal, the transformation of the workers into a revolutionary force for the overthrow of capitalism. Lenin wanted conditions to get worse, not better. In that way the bitterness of the industrial proletariat would increase, and so bring revolution nearer.

* Although Lenin despised the moderate, reformist intelligentsia, he argued, nonetheless, that it was only from that intellectual class that the leaders of revolution in Russia could be drawn. He set down his ideas on this theme in his pamphlet, *What is to be Done?*, published in 1902. The following extract is a key passage from it:

1 The history of every country teaches us that by its own ability the working class can attain only a trade-unionist self-consciousness, that is to say, an appreciation of the need to fight the bosses, to wrest from the government this or that legislative enactment for
5 the benefit of the workers. The Socialist [Communist] doctrine, on the other hand, is the outgrowth of those philosophical, historical and economic theories which had been developed by the representatives of the well to do, the intellectuals.
  By their social origin, Marx and Engels, the founders of
10 modern scientific socialism, were themselves members of the bourgeois intelligentsia. Similarly, in Russia, the theoretical principles of Social Democracy originated independently of the unconscious strivings of the labouring classes. They were a natural and inevitable result of the development of the ideas of the
15 revolutionary socialist intellectuals.
  The blind unfolding of the labour movement can lead only to the permeation of that movement with a bourgeois ideology, because the unconscious growth of the labour movement takes

the form of trade unionism, and trade unionism signifies the
20 mental enslavement of the workers to the bourgeoisie. Therefore
our task as Social Democrats is to oppose this blind process, to
divert the labour movement from the unconscious tendency of
trade unionism to march under the protective wing of the
bourgeoisie and to bring it under the influence of Social Democra-
25 cy instead.

Lenin wrote *What Is To Be Done?* as an answer to the followers of
Plekhanov, who were continuing to assert that success could be gained
only by a broad grouping of the progressive, reformist, anti-tsarist
elements in Russia. Lenin was adamant that the way forward could be
effectively organised only by a dedicated group of professional revolutionaries, whose unique insight into the dialectical revolutionary process entitled them alone to decide what was to be done. His reference to
the scientific nature of socialism was a crucial part of his argument.
Revolution for Lenin was not a haphazard affair; it was part of a natural
progression whose laws could be understood by scientific analysis. He
considered that Marx had, indeed, already provided this understanding. What remained now was for true Marxists to interpret and apply
the revolutionary message in Russia. This was why the workers could
not be left to themselves; only through the leadership of the truly
informed could the proletariat of Russia achieve victory in the class
war. In the Russian context, this leadership was supplied by the
revolutionary intelligentsia, which according to Lenin consisted, in
effect, of himself and those Marxists who agreed with him. Only they
could rescue the Russian working class and convert it to true socialism.
    * The dispute between Lenin and Plekhanov came to a head during
the second congress of the SD Party in 1903. Plekhanov tried to avoid
confrontation, but Lenin deliberately made an issue of who had the
right to membership of the Social Democratic Party. His aim was to
force the SDs to choose between Plekhanov's idea of a broad-based
party, open to all revolutionaries, and his own concept of a small,
tightly-knit and exclusive party of professional revolutionaries. The
congress was a heated affair, which often broke down into a series of
slanging matches over points of procedure. A deep divide developed
between Lenin and his *Iskra* co-editor, Martov. Their quarrel had as
much to do with personality as with politics. Martov believed that
behind Lenin's procedural tactics was a fierce determination to become
dictator of the party. The following was typical of their exchanges:

1 *Martov* – The more widely the title of 'member of the party' is
    spread, the better. We can only rejoice if every striker, every
    demonstrator, is able to declare himself a party member.
    Lenin – It is better that ten real workers should not call
5   themselves party members than that one chatterbox should have

the right and opportunity to be a member.

In a series of votes, the congress showed itself to be evenly divided between Lenin and Martov. However, after a particular set of divisions had gone in his favour, Lenin claimed that he and his supporters were the majority. This led to their being called Bolsheviks (from *bolshinstvo*, the Russian for majority). By the same token, Martov's group became known as Mensheviks (from *menshinstvo*, the Russian for minority). The Bolsheviks and Mensheviks began in 1903 as different factions within the Social Democratic Party. By 1912 they had become two distinct and opposed Marxist parties. Lenin deliberately emphasised the difference between himself and Martov by resigning from the editorial board of *Iskra* and starting his own journal, *Vyperod* (Forward), as an instrument for Bolshevik attacks upon the Mensheviks. A Bolshevik daily paper, *Pravda* (the Truth) was first published in 1912.

Initially, the main point dividing Bolsheviks and Mensheviks was simply one of procedure. However, following the split in 1903 the differences between them hardened into a set of opposed attitudes. These can be illustrated in tabulated form:

Menshevik	Bolshevik
Revolution	
Russia not yet ready for proletarian revolution – the bourgeois stage had to occur first	Bourgeois and proletarian stages could be telescoped into one
The party	
Mass organisation – membership open to all revolutionaries	Tight-knit organisation of professional revolutionaries – restricted membership
Discipline	
Open, democratic discussion within the party – decisions to be arrived at by votes of members	Authority to be exercised by the Central Committee of the party – this described as 'democratic centralism'
Strategy	
Alliance with all other revolutionary and bourgeois liberal parties – support of trade unions in pursuing better wages and conditions for workers	Rejection of co-operation with other parties – dismissed struggle for improved conditions as playing into hands of bourgeoisie – aimed to turn workers into revolutionaries

* Since the Bolsheviks ultimately gained power in 1917, there is an understandable tendency to consider Lenin's interpretation of revolution as more perceptive or realistic than that of the Mensheviks. However, care should be taken not to allow the use of hindsight to exaggerate the accuracy of Lenin's judgements or the significance of his role during the pre-revolutionary years. The later success of Bolshevism in the October Revolution has tempted many writers to overstate the importance of Lenin as a Russian revolutionary in the period leading up to 1917. For example, Trotsky, who joined Lenin in 1917 after having been a Menshevik, argued in his later writings that the Bolsheviks in the pre-1917 period had been systematically preparing the ground for revolution. Nevertheless, the truth is that during the years 1904 to 1917 Lenin was largely absent from Russia; his visits were rare and fleeting. Although he continued while in exile to issue a constant stream of instructions to his followers, the Bolsheviks played only a minor role in events in Russia before 1914. The 1905 Revolution took them by surprise. They were not involved in its early stages, and gained little from their belated attempt to exploit the situation. They tended to be regarded by the police authorities as one of the extremist groups who were not a major challenge to the tsarist system. Furthermore, it is estimated that in the pre-1914 period the numerical strength of the Bolsheviks varied between 5000 and 10,000, and that even in February 1917 it was no more than 25,000. Before 1917, the Mensheviks invariably outnumbered their Bolshevik rivals.

Numbers, of course, are not everything. Determination is arguably more important. Whatever the apparent lack of influence of Lenin's Bolsheviks before 1917, the fact is that when a revolutionary situation developed in 1917 it was they who proved the best prepared to seize the opportunity to take over government. That in itself is testimony to the real strength of the revolutionary party that Lenin had created.

5 The Liberals

There was never a single liberal party in tsarist Russia. Liberalism as a term is usually applied to those groups who genuinely wanted political or social change, but who believed that this could be achieved by reforming rather than destroying the tsarist system. The land reforms of Alexander II, which had led to the spread of the *zemstva*, had helped to create a progressive middle class in the countryside. This development had been matched in the urban areas. The economic boom of the 1890s saw the rapid development of a small but ambitious class of industrialists, lawyers and financiers. It was among such social groups that liberal ideas for the modernising of Russia began to take hold. There was also often a strong national element in Russian liberalism. The national minorities viewed the liberal movement as a means of expressing their wish to be independent of Russian imperial control.

Two principal liberal parties came to prominence in the pre-1914 period – the Octobrists and the Kadets.

a) The Octobrists

This group dated from the issuing of the tsar's manifesto of October 1905, which established the duma. The Octobrists were moderates who were basically loyal to the tsar and his government. They believed in the maintenance of the Russian Empire and regarded the manifesto and the establishment of the duma as going far enough in the direction of constitutional reform. The Octobrists were mainly drawn from the larger commercial, industrial and landowning interests. Their leading members were Guchkov, a factory owner, and Rodzianko, a large landowner, both of whom were later to play a leading part in the Provisional Government of 1917 (see page 85). How relatively limited the Octobrists were in their aims can be gauged from their programme, issued in November 1905. It called for:

> 1 . . . unity amongst those who sincerely want the peaceful renewal
> of Russia and the triumph of law and order in the country, who
> reject both stagnation and revolution and who recognise the need
> for the establishment of a strong and authoritative regime, which,
> 5 together with the representatives of the people, could bring peace
> to the country through constructive legislative work.

The limited objectives of the Octobrists led to their being dismissed by revolutionaries as bourgeois reactionaries. This is not wholly accurate. In the dumas, the Octobrists frequently voiced serious criticisms of the short-sightedness or incompetence of the tsarist government.

b) The Kadets (KDs)

The Kadet Party also came into being at the time of the 1905 Revolution. The title Kadets was a shortened form of Constitutional Democrats. They were also known as 'the Party of the People's Freedom'. This was the liberal group with the largest following. The Kadets wanted Russia to develop as a constitutional monarchy, in which the powers of the tsar would be restricted by a democratically-elected constituent (national) assembly. The creation of such a representative body, empowered to settle Russia's outstanding social, political and economic problems, became the major objective of all Russian liberals. Lenin scorned such an aim as typical of the political naivety of bourgeois liberals, but there is no doubt that the dream of a constituent assembly remained a source of excitement and inspiration to Russian reformers in the period before the 1917 Revolution.

Among the other widesweeping reforms demanded by the Kadets in

1905 were full equality and civil rights for all citizens, the ending of censorship, the abolition of redemption payments on land, the recognition of trade unions and the right to strike, and the introduction of universal, free education. The Kadets were the party of the liberal *intelligentsia*, containing progressive landlords, the smaller industrial entrepreneurs, and members of the professions. Academics were prominent in the party, as typified by the Kadet leader, Paul Milyukov, who was a professor of history. The Kadets became the major opposition voice in the first duma and were instrumental in forming the Provisional Government following the February Revolution in 1917.

6 The 1905 Revolution

a) Background

The situation created by the government's policy of political repression since 1881 was graphically described by Leo Tolstoy, the great Russian novelist and philosopher, in an open address to Nicholas II in 1902:

1 Russia lives under emergency legislation, and that means without any lawful guarantees. The armies of the secret police are continuously growing in numbers. The prisons and penal colonies are overcrowded with thousands of convicts and political prison-
5 ers, among whom the industrial workers are now included. The censorship issues the most meaningless interdictions [bans]. At no previous time have the religious persecutions been so frequent and so cruel as they are today. In all the cities and industrial centres soldiers are employed and equipped with live ammunition
10 to be sent out against the people. Yet this strenuous and terrible activity of the government results only in the growing impoverishment of the rural population, of those 100 million souls on whom the power of Russia is founded, and who, in spite of ever increasing budgets, are faced with famine which has become a
15 normal condition. A similar normal condition is the general dissatisfaction of all classes with the government and their open hostility against it. Autocracy is a superannuated form of government that may suit the needs of a Central African tribe, but not those of the Russian people, who are increasingly assimilating the
20 culture of the rest of the world. That is why it is impossible to maintain this form of government except by violence.

The bleak picture that Tolstoy painted did not necessarily mean that confrontation, still less revolution, had to come. After all, if oppression is resolutely applied it effectively prevents the forces of opposition growing to the point where they can confront government. Historians are coming increasingly to the view that what weakened the tsarist regime in the period before 1917 was not its tyranny but its incompetence. It is certainly true that the crisis which occurred in Russia in 1905 was in large measure due to the mishandling of the situation by the tsar and his government. This was shown by the speed with which the government reasserted its authority once it had recovered its nerve.

What made the events of 1905 a significant threat to the tsarist government was that for the first time it was faced by a combination of the three main opposition classes in Russia – the industrial workers, the peasantry, and the reformist middle class. This was the broad-based revolt that most revolutionaries had been awaiting, yet when it came it was accidental rather than planned. Despite the efforts of the various revolutionary parties to politicise events, the strikes and demonstrations in the pre-1905 period had been the result of economic rather than political factors. They had been a reaction to industrial recession and bad harvests. It was the tsarist regime's ill-judged policies that turned the disturbances into a direct challenge to its own authority.

b) The Course of Events

The 1905 Revolution began with what has become known as Bloody Sunday. On 22 January, Father Gapon, an Orthodox priest and *Okhrana* double-agent, attempted to lead a peaceful march of workers and their families to the Winter Palace in St Petersburg. The intention was to present a loyal petition to the tsar, begging him to use his royal authority to alleviate their desperate conditions. However, the march induced panic in the police authorities in the capital. The marchers were fired upon and were charged by cavalry. There are no precise figures, either of the number of marchers or of those killed, but the casualties seem to have amounted to hundreds. Although Nicholas II had been absent from St Petersburg at the time, the killings were depicted by opponents of the tsarist regime as a deliberate massacre of unarmed petitioners. Bloody Sunday gravely damaged the traditional image of the tsar as the 'Little Father', the special guardian of the Russian people.

The immediate reaction to the event was a nationwide outbreak of disorder, which increased as the year went on. Strikes occurred in all the cities and major towns. Terrorism against government officials and landlords, much of it organised by the SRs, spread through the countryside. The situation was made worse by Russia's humiliation in the war against Japan. The government was blamed for Russia's defeat, which occasioned further outrages, including the assassination of Plehve by SR terrorists. One newspaper reported that:

1 Hundreds of buildings, worth several millions of roubles, have been destroyed. All the buildings have been razed to the ground on some enormous estates. Many houses have been burnt down

without reference to the relations which had existed between the
5 peasants and the landowners or the latter's political views.

An important factor in the dissatisfaction of the peasants was their fear
that the government was about to seize the property of those peasant
families who had failed to pay off the mortgages taken out in the
immediate post-emancipation years (see page 13). The unrest and the
government's difficulties in containing it encouraged the national
minorities to assert themselves. Georgia declared itself an independent
state. Witte remarked:

1 [Non-Russians], seeing this great upheaval, lifted their heads and
decided that the time was ripe for the realisation of their dreams
and desires. The Poles wanted autonomy, the Jews wanted equal
rights, and so on. All of them longed for the destruction of the
5 system of deliberate oppression which embittered their lives. And
on top of everything, the army was in an ugly mood.

* In May, the Kadets, led by Milyukov, persuaded the majority of
the liberal groups to join them in forming a 'Union of Unions', with a
view to organising an alliance between themselves and the broad masses
of peasants and workers. A 'Union of Unions' declaration was issued:

1 All means are admissible in the face of the terrible menace
contained in the very fact of the continued existence of the
present government: and every means must be tried. We appeal
to all groups, to all parties, all organised unions, all private
5 groups, and we say with all our strength, with all the means at our
disposal, you must hasten the removal of the gang of robbers that
is now in power, and put in its place a constituent assembly.

During the summer, there came the still more disturbing news for
the tsarist authorities of mutinies in the army and navy. In June, the
crew of the battleship *Prince Potemkin* murdered their officers and
deserted their squadron by sailing out of Russian waters. The end of the
Russo-Japanese War in August did little to ease the situation. Indeed,
Witte feared that the returning troops would join the revolution 'and
then everything would collapse'. By the autumn, the industrial unrest
had grown into a general strike. It was in this atmosphere that a
development of particular significance occurred. In a number of cities,
most notably in St Petersburg and Moscow, workers formed themselves
into an elected soviet (Russian for council). The soviets began as
organisations to represent the workers' demands for better conditions,
but their potential as bases for political agitation was immediately
recognised by revolutionaries. The Menshevik, Lev Trotsky, became
chairman of the St Petersburg soviet and organiser of the general strike
in the capital.

*By October the tsar was faced by the most united opposition in Romanov history. It was at this critical juncture that the regime began to show the sense of purpose that it had so far lacked. Concession was unavoidable, but by giving ground the government intended to divide the opposition forces which confronted it. The liberals were the first to be placated by the granting of a duma. On Witte's advice, the tsar issued the October Manifesto in which he accepted the creation of a legislative (law-making) duma. This was a considerable constitutional advance on his offer a month earlier of a purely consultative assembly. Since the manifesto also contained a promise to introduce a range of civil rights, including freedom of speech, assembly and worship, and the legalising of trade unions, the liberals could claim a remarkable success for their action. Their appetite for reform was satisfied, at least temporarily. The peasants were the next to be bought off by an announcement in November that the mortgage repayments which had so troubled them were to be progressively reduced and then abolished altogether. The response was an immediate drop in the number of land-seizures by the peasants and a decline in the general lawlessness in the countryside.

Having won over the liberals and peasants, the government was now seriously opposed by only one major group – the industrial workers. Here the policy was one not of concession but of suppression. The government felt strong enough to attempt to crush the soviets. Despite the threatened mutinies earlier in the year, the troops who returned from the Far East at the end of the war proved loyal enough to be used against the strikers. After a five-day siege, the headquarters of the St Petersburg soviet were stormed and the ringleaders, including Trotsky, were arrested. The suppression of the Moscow soviet was even more violent. Lenin, who had been slow to take advantage of the 1905 Revolution, arrived in Moscow in December, only in time to witness the flames of the gutted soviet buildings.

c) Significance

It is a remarkable feature of the 1905 Revolution how minor a role was played by the revolutionaries. Hardly any of them were in St Petersburg or Moscow when it began. Revolution occurred in spite, rather than because of them. With the exception of Trotsky, none of the SDs made an appreciable impact on the course of events. This has led many historians to doubt whether the events of 1905 merit being called a revolution. They further point to the fact that in a number of important respects tsardom emerged from the disturbances stronger rather than weaker. In spite of its disastrous failure to win the war against Japan, which occasioned massive protest throughout Russia and united the classes in opposition, the tsarist regime survived 1905 relatively unscathed. The mutinies in the armed services, which had been the most threatening development, did not spread and did not continue after the war. Loyal troops returned to destroy the soviets. The readiness with which the liberals and the peasants accepted the government's political and economic bribes indicated that neither of those groups was genuinely ready for revolution. It is true that the tsar appeared to grant significant concessions in the October Manifesto, but these were expedients rather than real reforms. The duma was not intended to be, nor did it become, a limitation on the tsar's autocratic powers. This was evident from the Fundamental Laws, which Nicholas II promulgated in 1906:

1 The Sovereign Emperor possesses the initiative in all legislative matters. The Fundamental Laws may be subject to revision in the State Council and the State Duma only on His initiative. The Sovereign Emperor ratifies the laws. No law can come into force
5 without his approval.

The lesson of 1905 was that as long as the tsarist government kept its nerve and the army remained basically loyal, the forces of opposition would not be strong enough to mount a serious challenge. The events of 1905 also raised doubts about the extent to which the liberals wanted change in Russia. Few liberals enjoyed their experience of mixing with the workers during the Revolution. They found proletarian coarseness unattractive and were frightened by the primitive forces they had helped to unleash. One middle-class proprietor, who had thrown his house open to the strikers, remarked on the difficulty of sustaining his belief in the goodness of people who abused his hospitality by mauling his daughters and spitting on his carpet. Peter Struve, who had been a Marxist before joining the Kadets in 1905, spoke for all frightened liberals when he said 'Thank God for the tsar, who has saved us from the people'.

Trotsky's later reflections on the character of the 1905 Revolution provides an apt summary of its essential characteristics:

1 The events of 1905 were a prologue to the two revolutions of 1917. The Russo-Japanese war had made tsarism totter. Against the background of a mass movement the liberal bourgeoisie had frightened the monarchy with its opposition. The workers had
5 organised independently of the bourgeoisie in soviets. Peasant uprisings to seize the land occurred throughout the country. Not only the peasants, but also the revolutionary parts of the army tended towards the soviets. However, all the revolutionary forces were then going into action for the first time, lacking experience
10 and confidence. The liberals backed away from the revolution exactly at the moment when it became clear that to shake tsardom would not be enough, it must be overthrown. This sharp break of

the bourgeoisie with the people, in which the bourgeoisie carried with it considerable circles of the democratic intelligentsia, made
15 it easier for the monarchy to differentiate within the army, separating out the loyal units, and to make a bloody settlement with the workers and peasants. Although with a few broken ribs, tsarism came out of the experience of 1905 alive and strong enough.

7 The Dumas 1906–14

There were four dumas in the years between the 1905 Revolution and the February Revolution of 1917. The election of deputies to the first two dumas was based on a complicated system of electoral colleges, which were meant to represent the different social classes roughly in proportion to their size. The government imposed a much more restrictive system for the elections to the third and fourth dumas. The four elections produced the following results:

Party or group	First duma 1906	Second duma 1907	Third duma 1907–12	Fourth duma 1912–17
SDs (Mensheviks)	18	47	–	–
SDs (Bolsheviks)	–	–	19	15
SRs	–	37	–	–
Trudoviks★	136	104	13	10
Kadets	182	91	54	53
Octobrists	17	42	154	95
Progressists★★	27	28	28	41
Rightists★★★	8	10	147	154
National parties	60	93	26	22
Others	–	50	–	42
	448	518	441	432

★ The SRs as a party officially boycotted the elections to the first duma, but stood as *Trudoviks* (labourists).
★★ The Progressists were a party of businessmen who favoured moderate reform.
★★★ The Rightists were not a single party; they represented a range of conservative views from right of centre to extreme reaction.

a) The First Duma, April–June 1906

The high hopes of the liberals that the granting of the duma marked a real constitutional advance were dimmed even before it first met.

Having survived the challenge of 1905, the tsarist regime quickly recovered its confidence. Early in 1906, it successfully negotiated a substantial loan from France. This lessened the likelihood of the duma being able to exercise a financial hold over the government. A greater limitation on the duma's influence was the tsar's promulgation of the Fundamental Laws, which was timed to coincide with the opening of the duma. In addition to declaring that 'Supreme Autocratic Power' belonged to the tsar, the Laws announced that the duma would be composed of two chambers; one would be the elected duma, the other would be a state council, the majority of whose members would be appointed by the tsar. The existence of a second chamber with the power of veto deprived the elected duma of any genuine legislative control. Taken together with the declaration that no law could come into being without the tsar's approval, these restrictions made it clear that the tsarist regime had no intention of allowing the concessions it had made in 1905 to diminish its absolute authority.

The result was that the duma met in a mood of bitterness. The elections had returned a duma that was dominated by the liberal and reformist parties. They immediately voiced their anger at what they regarded as the government's reneging on its promises. They demanded that the rights and powers of the duma be increased. Goremykin, the chief minister, told them that their demands were 'inadmissible' and Nicholas II was reported as saying, 'Curse the duma. It is all Witte's doing'. After two months of acrimonious wrangling, the tsar ordered the duma to be dissolved. In frustration, 200 Kadet and *Trudovik* deputies reassembled at Vyborg in Finland where they drew up an 'Appeal', urging the people of Russia to defy their government by non-payment of taxes and refusal to obey conscription orders. The Vyborg Appeal was an ill-considered move. The response from the population was not national passive disobedience but scattered violence. This provided the government with a ready excuse for retaliation. The tsar appointed Stolypin as chief minister to act as his strong man. The Vyborg group were arrested and debarred from re-election to the duma. This was the prelude to Stolypin's embarking on a policy of fierce repression, which he sustained until his assassination in 1911. Martial law was proclaimed and a network of courts-martial, with wide-reaching powers, was used to quell disturbances. There were so many hangings (over 2500 between 1906 and 1911) that the executioner's noose became known throughout Russia as 'Stolypin's necktie'.

b) The Second Duma, February–June 1907

The Kadet failure in 1906 had important long-term effects. Although the Kadet Party survived under the leadership of Milyukov, it never really recovered from its humiliation. The liberal cause had discredited itself, thus allowing both the left and the right to capitalise politically by arguing from their different standpoints that the future of Russia lay either in socialist revolution or extreme reaction.

The immediate result was that in the elections for the second duma the number of Kadet seats was halved. The beneficiaries were the SDs and the SRs, who between them returned over 80 deputies. This increase in the radical element meant that the second duma was no less combative than the first had been. Since the right were also more strongly represented than in the previous assembly, there was considerable disagreement within the duma as well as between it and the government. Stolypin, who, despite his stern repression of social disorder, was willing to work with the duma in introducing necessary reforms, found his land programme strenuously opposed. The tsar was particularly incensed to learn of the duma's criticism of the government's administration of the army. Amid scenes of disorder, following government accusations that the SD and SR deputies were engaging in subversion, the second duma was dissolved after barely three months' existence.

c) The Third Duma, November 1907–June 1912

Despite the opposition shown by the first two dumas, the tsar made no attempt to dispense with the duma altogether. There were two reasons for this. One was that under the terms of his October Manifesto of 1905 he was obliged to maintain the duma as part of the constitution. This in itself would not have deterred him from scrapping it, but he had an ulterior motive. Foreign policy considerations prompted him to project an image of Russia as a democratic nation. He was advised by his foreign ministers, who at this time were negotiating agreements with France and Britain (see page 30), that Russia's new allies were considerably impressed by existence of an apparently representative national assembly.

The second reason was that the duma had been rendered docile by the government's doctoring of the electoral system, so as to return an assembly from which the critics of tsardom were largely excluded. This had been achieved by Stolypin's introduction of new electoral laws which greatly restricted the franchise, thereby reducing the peasant vote. That he had made the changes in direct contravention of the Fundamental Laws showed his and the government's contempt for constitutional procedures. His new franchise laws effectively limited the vote to the propertied classes. In the election to the third duma, only one in six of the male population had the right to vote. The peasants and industrial workers were virtually excluded. The consequence was (as the table on page 50 shows) that the third and fourth dumas were heavily dominated by the right-wing parties, a reversal of the position in the first and second dumas in which the radical parties had held a large majority.

With the balance of the parties redressed in this way, Stolypin was able to develop relatively harmonious relations with the third duma, which enabled him to pursue his land reforms without opposition from the deputies (see page 28). This is not to say that the duma was entirely subservient. It exercised its right to question ministers and to discuss state finances. It also used its committee system to make important proposals for the modernisation of the armed services. The duma took the initiative in developing schemes of national insurance for industrial workers, which were as progressive as any in contemporary Europe.

c) The Fourth Duma, November 1912–August 1914

It was Stolypin's tragedy that his abilities were never fully appreciated by the regime he tried to serve. It is especially revealing of the regime's mentality that it tended to regard talent in its ministers as dangerous. Following Stolypin's murder in 1911, the tsar appointed a series of nonentities and incompetents to run his government. Since they lacked political imagination, their only course was further repression. An intensification of the anti-Jewish pogroms was one expression of this. Between 1911 and 1914 the regime's terror tactics were part cause, part effect, of a dramatic increase in public disorder, which gradually returned to the proportions of 1905. The number of strikes listed as 'political' by the Ministry of Trade and Industry rose from 24 in 1911 to 2401 in 1914. The following report from a Moscow *Okhrana* agent in 1912 was typical of the news reaching the government:

1 There has never been so much tension. People can be heard speaking of the government in the sharpest and most unbridled tones. Many say that the 'shooting' of the Lena workers recalls the 'shooting' of the workers at the Winter Palace of January 9
5 1905. Influenced by questions in the duma and the speeches which they called forth there, public tension is increasing still more. It is a long time since even the extreme left has spoken in such a way, since there have been references in the duma to 'the necessity of calling a Constituent Assembly and overthrow the
10 present system by the united strength of the proletariat'.

* The mention of the Lena workers was a reference to the notorious incident that occurred in 1912 in the Lena Goldfields in Siberia. Demands from the miners there for better pay and conditions were resisted by the employers who appealed to the police to arrest the strikers' leaders as criminals. The issue thus became the much larger one of trade union rights in Russia. When the police moved into Lena the strikers closed ranks and the situation rapidly worsened, resulting in troops firing on and killing or wounding a large number of miners. The *Okhrana* appeared to have acted as *agents provocateurs* in order to identify the ringleaders of the strike. The agent's report is also significant in its reference to the protests in the fourth duma, which although later described by post-1917 revolutionaries as having been a cowed, ineffectual, body was obviously capable of making spirited protest. The truth was that many moderates in the duma had begun to despair that the government would respond adequately or realistically to the problems confronting Russia. Guchkov told the Octobrist Party conference in 1913:

1 [The] attempt made by the Russian public, as represented by our party, to effect a peaceful, painless transition from the old condemned system to a new order has failed. Let those in power make no mistake about the temper of the people; let them not
5 take outward indications of prosperity as a pretext for lulling themselves into security. Never were the Russian people so profoundly revolutionised by the actions of the government, for day by day faith in the government is steadily waning, and with it is waning faith in the possibility of a peaceful issue of the crisis.

In the following year the duma expressed its sense of impending catastrophe in a formal resolution:

1 The Ministry of the Interior systematically scorns public opinion and ignores the repeated wishes of the new legislature. The duma considers it pointless to express any new wishes in regard to internal policy. The Ministry's activities arouse dissatisfaction
5 among the broad masses who have hitherto been peaceful. Such a situation threatens Russia with untold dangers.

After 1917, it was usual for historians to follow the lead of Bolshevik critics in dismissing the later dumas as having been merely rubber stamps of government policy. However, modern scholars tended to be less critical. They refer to the dumas' frequent and searching criticisms of government policy, their productive work in such areas as education and state insurance, and suggest that it was only the ineptitude of the tsarist government that prevented the dumas from making a greater contribution to the development of Russian politics.

8 Conclusion

The period 1881–1914 may be regarded as a time of lost opportunity for tsardom. The economic policies of Witte and Stolypin and the introduction of the duma were important advances in themselves, but they were not enough to alter the essentially reactionary character of the tsarist system. The attitude of the government towards reform remained hostile. The industrial spurt of the 1890s had offered an opportunity for Russia to modernise herself, but a sustained policy of modernisation required not simply economic progress but a commitment to political change as well. This the tsar was never willing to give. This would have mattered less if the system had operated efficiently. But the tsarist autocracy was both oppressive and inefficient, thereby alienating the progressive elements in society, which could see no possibility of real advance in Russia as long as government and administration remained in the hands of incompetents.

It was this that undermined the work of the few enlightened ministers such as Witte and Stolypin within the government. They were reformers but they were also loyalists. Indeed, it was their loyalty to the system that led them to consider reform as a way of lessening the opposition to it. The irony was that they were not trusted by the representatives of the very system they were trying to preserve. It is for this reason that historians have suggested that in failing to recognise the true worth of Witte and Stolypin, the tsarist regime unwittingly threw away its last chance of survival. By 1914, all the signs were that imperial Russia was heading towards a major confrontation between intransigent tsardom and the forces of change. It was to be the war of 1914–17 that would determine what form that conflict would take.

Making notes on 'Opposition to Tsardom 1881–1914'

The groups who came to oppose tsardom during this period covered a wide political spectrum. One of your main aims in studying this chapter should be to gain an understanding of these shades of opinion. Another should be to continue your assessment of the way in which the tsarist regime handled the situation.

The following headings and questions are intended to provide a basis for analysis.

1.   Introductory Survey
1.1. The broad developments, 1881–1914
2.   The Populists
2.1. The place of the peasants
2.2. 'The People's Will'
3.   The Social Revolutionaries
3.1. The link between Populism and the SRs
3.2. Distinguish between the anarchist and revolutionary wings of the SRs
4.   The Social Democrats
4.1. The ideas of Karl Marx
4.2. Why was Marxism so attractive to Russian revolutionaries?

Answering essay questions on 'Opposition to Tsardom 1881–1914'

Chapters 3 and 4 complement each other. It is not possible to understand the nature of the opposition to tsardom without a knowledge of the social, economic and political themes introduced in chapter 3. Therefore, it is essential when preparing your essay answers to think about the material contained in both chapters.

It is advisable to concentrate on the main themes relating to the development of opposition; you are unlikely to be asked obscure questions in this area. It is especially important that you understand the basic political ideas advanced by the major revolutionaries. Lenin is a crucial figure in this respect, and you should aim to familiarise yourself with his thinking. A grasp of the subsequent history of Russia down to 1924 and, indeed, beyond, requires a working knowledge of Lenin's concept of revolution.

Consider the following questions, which cover the main themes relating to the opposition to tsardom:

1. '"The importance of Populism in Russia lay in its methods, not its objectives." Discuss.'
2. 'Why did the SD Party split into Bolshevik and Menshevik factions in 1903?'

3. 'How serious a threat to tsardom was the 1905 Revolution?'
4. 'In what ways did Lenin adjust Marxist ideas to make them fit the Russian context before 1914?'
5. 'Did the ideas of the Russian liberals offer a genuine alternative to tsarist autocracy in the period before 1914?'
6. ' "Unlike the first and second dumas, the third and fourth dumas were nothing more than a talking shop.' Discuss.'

Remember, as always, that when you prepare an essay plan your aim must be to meet the precise terms of the question. Your notes are not in themselves an answer: they provide only the raw material.

Consider question 3. The requirement is to determine how closely the tsarist regime came to being overthrown. Draw up a list of the opposition forces in 1905. Rank them according to their relative strength and importance. Then list the resources that the tsarist regime had at its disposal. Now ask yourself the question, 'Was the opposition powerful enough to be a real threat when set against the basic strength of the tsarist regime in 1905?' If you then pose yourself further supplementary questions you will find that an answer to the basic essay question will start to form. 'How significant was the coming together of the three social groups – liberals, peasants and industrial workers?' 'Was their union planned or merely accidental and superficial?'

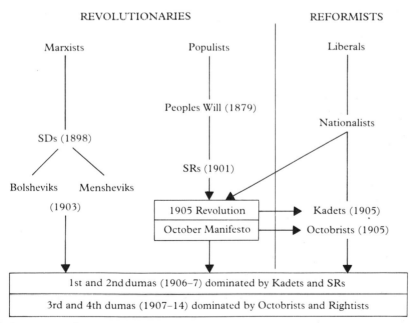

Summary – Opposition to Tsardom 1881–1914

'How soon did the regime recover its nerve?' 'Did not the events show that tsardom possessed sufficient political and military strength either to buy off or to smash the opposition?'

Another helpful way into thinking about this question is to ask yourself whether the opposition really wanted the overthrow of the system or merely its reform. Your notes should provide you with the material to answer all these questions. It would be appropriate to refer to Trotsky's observations on 1905. He emphasised the inexperience and lack of confidence of the revolutionaries, stressed how the liberals had been frightened of revolution, and laid particular weight on the government's retention of the loyalty of the armed services. Since these ideas come from someone who was both an opponent of the regime and a prominent participant in the events of 1905, they merit a central place in your answer.

Source-based questions on 'Opposition to Tsardom 1881–1914'

1 Lenin's Revolutionary Ideas
Study the extract from Lenin's writings on pages 40–41, and then answer the following questions:
a) What do you understand Lenin to mean by saying (line 1) that 'by its own ability the working class can attain only a trade-unionist self-consciousness'? (6 marks)
b) Comment on the significance of Lenin's statement (line 11) that 'in Russia, the theoretical priciples of Social Democracy originated independently of the unconscious strivings of the labouring classes'. (7 marks)
c) Using your own knowledge and the evidence in the extracts, examine Lenin's concept of the role of the *intelligentsia* in revolution. (8 marks)

2 The 1905 Revolution
Read the extract from Tolstoy's address on page 49 and from Trotsky's reflections on pages 49–50. Then answer the following questions:
a) What features of tsarist repression does Tolstoy emphasise in this extract? (4 marks)
b) Examine the implications of Tolstoy's description of the Russian autocracy as 'a superannuated form of government' (line 17). (5 marks)
c) Using your own knowledge, assess the accuracy of Trotsky's explanation of the eventual withdrawal of the liberals from the 1905 Revolution. (7 marks)

d) How closely do the descriptions given by Tolstoy and Trotsky agree in their analyses of the forces opposing tsardom? (8 marks)

3 The Dumas

Study the table on page 50 and the extracts on pages 53–54, and then answer the following questions:

a) What does the table of election results reveal about the political shifts in the duma between 1906 and 1912? (7 marks)
b) According to the *Okhrana* agent's report on page 53, what part did the duma play in the creation of social tension in Russia? (3 marks)
c) To what extent do Guchkov's speech and the duma resolution on page 54 present similar pictures of the political situation in Russia before 1914? (7 marks)
d) Assess the strengths and weaknesses of each of the three sources as evidence for the role of the dumas between 1906 and 1914. (9 marks)

CHAPTER 5

War and Revolution 1914–17

1 Russia's Entry into the First World War

There were no clear signs that the tsarist government wanted war in 1914. Russia's experience ten years earlier against Japan had made her wary of putting herself at risk again, and her foreign policy after 1905 had been essentially defensive. She had joined France and Britain in the Triple Entente as a means of safeguarding herself against the alliance of the Central Powers, Germany and Austria-Hungary. However, the events that followed the assassination in June 1914 of Franz Ferdinand, the heir to the Austro-Hungarian throne, by Serbian nationalists made it impossible for Russia to avoid being drawn into a European conflict.

By tradition, Russia was the protector of the Slav peoples of the Balkans. With the decline of Turkey, the old enemy, in the nineteenth century, Austria-Hungary was seen by Russia as the new threat. Sazonov, the tsar's foreign secretary in 1914, described the link between the commitment to defend Slav nationalism in the Balkans and Russia's long-standing strategic interests:

1 Russia's historical mission – the emancipation of the Christian peoples of the Balkan peninsula from the Turkish yoke – was almost fulfilled by the beginning of the twentieth century. Although these younger countries no longer needed the guar-
5 dianship of Russia, they were not strong enough to dispense with her help in the event of any attempt upon their national existence by warlike Teutonism [Germanic expansionism]. Serbia in particular was exposed to this danger, having become the object of the decorously concealed covetousness of Austrian diplomacy.
10 Russia's sole and unchanging object was to see that those Balkan peoples should not fall under the influence of powers hostile to her. The ultimate aim of Russian policy was to obtain free access to the Mediterranean, and to be in a position to defend her Black Sea coasts against the threat of the irruption of hostile naval forces
15 through the Bosphorus.

A month after Franz Ferdinand's murder, Austria-Hungary, with German encouragement, declared war on Serbia. Russia still expected to be able to assert herself and oblige the Austrians to withdraw, without herself having to go to war. She hoped that by mobilising her army she would deter Austria from proceeding any further. This was not unrealistic. Despite Russia's defeat by Japan, her armies were still regarded as formidable. Germans often spoke of 'the Russian steamroller', a reference to the immense reserves of manpower on which it was calculated that Russia could draw.

* It was at this stage that the great length of her western frontier became a critical consideration. Russia had two basic mobilisation schemes, partial and full. 'Partial' involved contingency plans for a campaign in the south-west in defence of her Slav interests in the Balkans; 'full' involved plans for a general European war. Both forms of mobilisation were based on detailed railway timetabling aimed at transporting huge numbers of men and vast amounts of material. The complexity of the timetables meant that the adoption of one type of mobilisation ruled out the use of the other. The Russian fear in July 1914 was that if she mobilised only partially she would leave herself defenceless should Austria's ally, Germany, strike at Russia's East Prussian and Polish borders. On the other hand, full mobilisation might well appear to Germany as a deliberate provocation. The German government did, indeed, warn Sazonov that if Russia mobilised Germany would have to do the same. The fact was that, according to German contingency plans, if Russia mobilised war became unavoidable. The German 'Schlieffen Plan' was based on the concept of eliminating the danger to Germany of a two-front war against France and Russia by a lightning knock-out blow against France. Speed was of the essence. Germany could not play a game of diplomatic bluff; she had to strike first.

The French ambassador in St Petersburg at the time described the fateful Russian decision:

1 29th July . . . At eleven o'clock tonight, Basily [deputy director at the Russian Foreign Office] came to tell me that the imperious language used by the German Ambassador this afternoon has decided the Russian Government *(1)* to order this very night the
5 mobilisation of the 13 corps earmarked for operations against Austria-Hungary, *(2)* secretly to commence general mobilisation.

    These last words made me jump.

    'Isn't it possible for them to confine themselves – provisionally at any rate – to a partial mobilisation?'
10 'No. The question has just been gone into thoroughly by a council of our highest military officers. They have come to the conclusion that in the existing circumstances the Russian Government has no choice between partial and general mobilisation, as from the technical point of view a partial mobilisation could be
15 carried out only at the price of dislocating the entire machinery of general mobilisation. So if today we stopped at mobilising the 13 corps destined for operations against Austria and tomorrow Germany decided to give her ally military support, we should be powerless to defend ourselves on the frontiers of Poland and East
20 Prussia.'

The Russian mobilisation order, eventually signed by an uncertain tsar, had been intended as a defensive move, a diplomatic manoeuvre which would still leave Russia free to hold back from war. In the event, it proved to be the gesture that pushed the Central Powers over the edge. On 1 August Germany declared war on Russia. Four days later Austria-Hungary did the same.

2   Russia at War

Nicholas had had reservations about war with Germany. In July he had exchanged a series of personal telegrams with his cousin, Kaiser William II, regretting the growing crisis in Russo-German relations. However, once war had been declared, the tsar became wholly committed to it. By 1917 the war would prove to be the undoing of tsardom, but in 1914 the outbreak of hostilities greatly enhanced the tsar's position. Nicholas became the symbol of the nation's resistance in its hour of need. Watching the great crowds cheering the tsar as he formally announced that Russia was at war, the French ambassador remarked: 'To those thousands the tsar really is the autocrat, the absolute master of their bodies and souls.' At a special session of the duma, all the deputies, save for the five Bolshevik representatives, fervently pledged themselves to the national struggle.

It was the same story in all the warring countries. The socialist parties abandoned their policies and committed themselves to the national war effort. Lenin was bitter in his condemnation of those 'class traitors'. He called on all true revolutionaries 'to transform the imperialist war everywhere into a civil war'. But the prevailing mood in Russia and Europe was all against him. The early stages of the war were dark days for Lenin's Bolsheviks. Vilified as traitors and German agents for their opposition to the war, they were forced to flee or go into hiding. Lenin, who was already in exile in Poland, made his way with Austrian help into neutral Switzerland. Had the war gone well for Russia there is every reason to think that the Bolshevik Party would have withered and died.

★ But the war did not go well for Russia, and the reason was only partly military. The basic explanation for her decline and slide into revolution in 1917 was an economic one. Three years of total war were to prove too great a strain for the Russian economy to bear. War is a time when the character and structure of a society are put to the test in a particularly intense way. The longer the war lasts, the greater the test. During the years 1914–17, the political, social and economic institutions of Russia proved increasingly incapable of meeting the demands that war placed upon them. This does not prove that Russia was uniquely incompetent. The pressure of total war on all countries was immense and it should be remembered that of the five empires engaged in the First World War only one survived. The fact is that, however

Russia's potential for growth in 1914 is assessed, the demands of the total war which she entered in that year eventually proved too heavy for her existing structures to sustain. The impact of the war on Russia can be studied under four headings

a) Inflation

Such financial stability as Russia had achieved before 1914 was destroyed by the war. Between 1914 and 1917 over 17,000 million roubles were spent on the war effort. The national budget multiplied by nearly eight times during this period, from four million roubles in 1913 to 30 million in 1916. Increased taxation, domestic bank loans and heavy borrowing from abroad were resorted to but were only partially successful in supplying the capital Russia needed. The gold standard (the system by which currency is valued according to how much gold it can buy) was abandoned. This allowed the government to put more notes into circulation. While in the short-term this enabled wages to be paid and commerce to continue, in the long-term it made money practically worthless. The result was severe inflation, which became particularly acute in 1916.

*Prices**		*Notes in circulation**	
July 1914	100	July 1914	100
January 1915	130	January 1915	146
January 1916	141	January 1916	199
January 1917	398	January 1917	336

*To a base unit of 100.

In broad terms, between 1914 and 1916 average earnings doubled while the price of food and fuel quadrupled.

b) Food Supplies

To the growing problem of the price of food were added the difficulties relating to its production and distribution. Full-scale mobilisation took over 15 million men from the countryside during the course of the war.

Number of men mobilised into the Russian army

1914	*1915*	*1916*	*mid-1917*	
6.5	11.2	14.2	36.7	(millions)

Military needs led to the requisitioning of farm horses and a drastic cut in the supply of chemical fertilisers. It was difficult to maintain agricultural production in such circumstances. However, the decline in food production should not be exaggerated. During the first two years of the war grain production was maintained at a slightly higher rate than the average for the five years before 1915. It was not until 1916 that it began to fall. Part of the reason for this was that, since inflation made trading unprofitable, the peasants stopped marketing their produce and began to hoard their stocks. What made it still more difficult for the ordinary Russian to acquire regular supplies was that the army had first claim to the more limited amount of food that was produced. The armed services also had prior use of the transport system. The military commandeered the railways and the roads, with the result that food distribution to civilian areas was unreliable and inadequate.

Hunger bordering on famine became a constant reality for much of Russia during the war years. Shortages were at their worst in the towns and cities. Petrograd (the Russian name for St Petersburg, adopted for patriotic reasons soon after the war began) suffered particularly badly because of its remoteness from the food-producing regions and because of the large number of destitute refugees who swelled its population and increased the demand on its dwindling resources. The bitter irony was that despite the priority given to supplying the army the overall decline in food production meant that troop rations could not be maintained. In the first two years of the war the army managed to meet its cereal needs, but from 1916 serious shortages began to occur.

Daily bread ration (in pounds weight)

January 1916 2.7   December 1916 2.3   March 1917 1.8

c) Transport

It was the disruption of the transport system rather than the decline in food production that was the more significant cause of Russia's wartime privations. The growth of the railways, from 21,000 kilometres in 1881 to 70,000 in 1914, had been an impressive feature of Russia's economic development, but it did not prove adequate for the demands of war. The integrated character of a railway network means that even a minor hold-up somewhere can badly affect the whole system. The attempt to transport millions of troops and masses of supplies to the war fronts created unbearable pressures. Blocked lines and trains stranded by locomotive breakdown or lack of coal became increasingly common.

Less than two years after the war began, the Russian railway system had virtually collapsed. By 1916, 575 stations were no longer capable of handling freight. A graphic example of the confusion was provided by Archangel, the northern port through which the bulk of the allied supplies to Russia were sent. It was recorded that so great was the pile-up of undistributed goods that they sank into the ground beneath the weight of new supplies. Elsewhere there were frequent reports of food rotting in railway trucks that could not be moved. One of the tsar's wartime prime ministers later admitted: 'There were so many trucks blocking the lines that we had to tip some of them down the embankments to move the ones that arrived later.' Before the war Moscow had received an average of 2200 wagons of grain per month; by February 1917 this figure had dropped to below 700. The figures for Petrograd told a similar story; in February 1917 the capital received only 300 wagon-loads of grain.

d) The Army

The suffering that the food shortages and dislocated transport system caused might have been bearable had the news from the front been encouraging or had there been inspired leadership from the top. But, despite occasional military successes such as those achieved in 1916 under General Brusilov, the gains made were never enough to justify the appalling casualty lists. Over four million Russian troops were killed or wounded in the first year of the war. The enthusiasm and high morale of August 1914 had turned by 1916 into pessimism and defeatism. Ill-equipped and under-fed, the 'peasants in uniform' who composed the Russian army began to desert in increasing numbers. The army's priority use of the transport system became valueless once that system had begun to break down. Rodzyanko, the president of the duma, who undertook a special fact-finding study in 1916 of conditions in the army, reported dismally to the duma on the widespread disorganisation:

1 General Ruzsky complained to me of lack of ammunition and the
   poor equipment of the men. There was a great shortage of boots.
   The soldiers fought barefooted.
      The hospitals and stations of the Red Cross, which came under
5 my notice, were in excellent condition; but the war hospitals were
   disorganised. They were short of bandages and such things. The
   great evil was, of course, the lack of co-operation between the two
   organisations. At the front, one had to walk about ten or more
   versts from the war hospitals to those of the Red Cross. [One verst
10 equals two thirds of a mile.]
      The Grand Duke stated that he was obliged to stop fighting,
   temporarily for lack of ammunition and boots.
      There was plenty of material and labour in Russia. But as it
   stood then, one region had leather, another nails, another soles,
15 and still another cheap labour. The best thing to do would be to
   call a congress of the heads of the zemstvos and ask for their
   co-operation.

The clear implication in Rodzyanko's account was that the strong central leadership which the war effort desperately needed was not being provided. This was a view that became increasingly widespread. Nicholas had made the momentous decision in 1915 to assume direct command of Russia's armed services. It was a gesture intended to rally the nation around the tsar, but what it did was to make him personally responsible for Russia's performance in the war. Lack of success could no longer be blamed upon his appointees.

Care should be taken not to understate Russia's military capabilities. Modern research has undermined the notion that the Russian army was on the verge of collapse in 1917. Norman Stone, for example, dismisses the idea of a disintegrating army as a Bolshevik 'fabrication'. He also emphasises the vital role that Russia played as an ally of Britain and France in tying down the German army for three years on the eastern front. An interesting detail, indicating how far Russia was from absolute collapse in 1916, is that in that year Russia managed to produce more shells than Germany. To quote these findings is not to deny the importance of Russia's military crises, but it is to recognise that historians have traditionally tended to exaggerate Russia's military weakness in 1917.

3 The Growth of Political Opposition

Nonetheless, the picture of an incompetent tsar, unable to provide the inspiration that the nation required, was an image that all-important sections of the population came to see as a reflection of the barrenness of the tsarist system itself. It is worth noting at this point that the first moves in the February Revolution in 1917, the event that led to the fall of tsardom, were not to be made by the political revolutionaries. In fact, the Revolution was to be set in motion by those elements of Russian society which had been the most eager to rally to the tsar in 1914, but who, by the winter of 1916, were too wearied or outraged by his ineptitude to wish to save him.

In a gesture of patriotic solidarity with the tsar's government, the duma had accepted its prorogation in August 1914, but within a year Russia's poor showing in the war led to demands for its recall. Nicholas bowed before the pressure and allowed the duma to reassemble in August 1915. One major political mistake of the tsar and his ministers was their refusal to co-operate fully with the non-governmental organisations such as the Union of *Zemstva* and the Union of Town Councils, which at the beginning of the war had been wholly willing to work with the government in the national war effort. These elected bodies formed a joint organisation, Zemgor, whose main commitment was to relief work among Russia's millions of war casualties. Zemgor's success in this field both highlighted the government's own failures and hinted that there might be a workable and democratic alternative to tsardom.

A similar political blindness characterised the tsar's dismissal of the duma's appeal to him to replace his palpably incompetent cabinet with 'a ministry of national confidence'. In rejecting this proposal, Nicholas destroyed the last opportunity he would have of retaining the support of the politically progressive parties. Milyukov, the Kadet leader, commented: 'They brushed aside the hand that was offered them. The conflict on the one hand between the representatives of the people and society on the other became an open breach'. Denied a direct voice in national policy, 236 out of the total of 422 duma deputies formed themselves into a 'Progressive Bloc' composed of the Kadets, the Octobrists, the Nationalists and the Party of Progressive Industrialists. The SRs did not formally join the Bloc but voted with it in all the duma divisions. Initially, the Bloc did not directly challenge the tsar's authority, but sought to persuade him to make concessions. However, as he and his government showed themselves increasingly incapable the Bloc became the focal point of political resistance.

* The government continued to shuffle its ministers in the hope of creating political stability and administrative efficiency. In the two years 1915–16, there were four changes of prime minister, three new foreign secretaries, three different ministers of defence, and a succession of six interior ministers. It was all to no avail. None of them was up to the task. The description by the British ambassador in Petrograd of one of the premiers, Sturmer, might have been fairly applied to all the tsar's wartime ministers:

1 Possessed of only a second-class mind, having no experience of statesmanship, concerned exclusively with his own personal interests, and distinguished by his capacity to flatter and his extreme ambition, he owed his appointment to the fact that he
5 was a friend of Rasputin and enjoyed the support of the crowd of intriguers around the empress.

The reference to Rasputin introduces the individual on whom the accumulated hatred of the tsarist system came to be focused. Rasputin was a self-ordained holyman, who was notorious for his sexual excesses. As far back as 1907 he had inveigled himself into the imperial court on the strength of his reputation as a faith healer. The tsarina, desperate to cure her haemophiliac son, Alexei, fell under Rasputin's spell and made him her *confidant*. Scandal inevitably followed. Alexandra's German nationality had made her suspect and unpopular since the outbreak of war, but she tried to ride out the storm. She would hear no ill of 'our dear friend' and obliged her husband to maintain Rasputin at court. Since Nicholas was away at military headquarters for long periods after 1915, it is barely an exaggeration to say that Alexandra and Rasputin effectively became the government of Russia. By any measure Rasputin's rise to prominence in Russia was an extraordinary story, but its

An opposition cartoon showing the tsar and tsarina under the control of Rasputin

true significance lay in the light it shed on the nature of tsarist government. Even the staunchest supporters of tsardom found it difficult to defend a system which allowed a nation in the hour of its greatest trial to fall under the sway of a debauched monk. In December 1916, in an attempt to save the monarchy, a group of aristocratic conspirators murdered him.

However, no matter how much the court and the right-wing elements might rejoice at the death of the upstart, the truth was that by the beginning of 1917 it was too late to save tsardom. The Rasputin scandal had been a bizarre symptom of the disease affecting Russian politics rather than the cause of it.

4 The February Revolution

The rising of February 1917 was not the first open move against the tsar or his government to have occurred. During the preceding year there had been a number of attempted palace *coups*. The assassination of Rasputin belonged to these. In the duma, the Octobrists had demanded the removal of unwanted ministers and generals. What made February 1917 different was the range of the opposition to the government and the speed with which events turned from a rising into a revolution. Rumours of the likelihood of serious public disturbances breaking out in Petrograd had been widespread since the beginning of the year. In January an *Okhrana* report stated:

1 There is a marked increase in hostile feelings among the peasants not only against the government but also against all other social groups. The proletariat of the capital is on the verge of despair. The mass of industrial workers are quite ready to let themselves
5 go to the wildest excesses of a hunger riot. The prohibition of all labour meetings, the closing of trade unions, the prosecution of men taking an active part in the sick benefit funds, the suspension of labour newspapers, and so on, make the labour masses, led by the more advanced and already revolutionary-minded elements,
10 assume an openly hostile attitude towards the Government and protest with all the means at their disposal against the continuation of the war.

About the same time, the president of the duma, Rodzyanko, warned the tsar that 'very serious outbreaks of unrest' were imminent. He added ominously, 'there is not one honest man left in your entourage; all the decent people have either been dismissed or left'. Nonetheless, it has to be kept in mind that nothing specific had happened up to February 1917 to make revolution inevitable. It was rather that February marked the stage at which the accumulated sufferings of the Russian people reached breaking point.

The Revolution occupied the period from 18 February to 4 March. A full-scale strike was started on 18 February by the employees at the Putilov steel works, the largest and most politically-active factory in Petrograd. During the next five days, the Putilov strikers were joined on the streets by growing numbers of disaffected workers, disturbed by rumours of a further cut in bread supplies. Later research has suggested that these rumours were exaggerated and that bread supplies were still sufficient for the capital's basic needs. However, in times of social unrest rumour often has the same power as fact.

23 February happened to be International Women's Day. This brought thousands of women onto the streets to join the protesters in demanding food and an end to the war. By 25 February, Petrograd was

paralysed by what amounted to a general strike. Factories were occupied and attempts by the police and mounted cossacks to disperse groups of workers were enfeebled by the growing sympathy for the demonstrators shown by those responsible for law and order. There was a great deal of confusion and little leadership or direction. Events which were later seen as having had major political significance took place in an atmosphere in which political protests were indistinguishable from the general outcry against food shortages and the privations of war.

The tsar, at his military headquarters at Mogilev, 400 miles from Petrograd, relied for news largely on the letters received from the tsarina, who was still in the capital. When he learned from her about the disturbances, whose seriousness she understated, Nicholas ordered the commander of the Petrograd garrison, General Khabalov, to restore order. Khabalov, who had been appointed commander only a week before, cabled back that, with the various contingents of the police and militia either fighting each other or joining the demonstrators on the streets and his own garrison troops showing open insubordination, he doubted that the situation could be contained. Khabalov had been quite willing to take drastic measures; he had wanted the government to declare martial law in Petrograd, which would have given him the power to use unlimited force against the demonstrators. But such was the breakdown of ordinary life in the capital that the martial law proclamation could not even be printed, let alone distributed or enforced. More serious still, by 26 February all but a few thousand of the original 150,000 garrison troops had deserted or mutinied. In addition, a battalion of troops sent from the front under General Ivanov had nearly all deserted by the time they reached the outskirts of Petrograd.

Faced with this near-hopeless situation, Rodzyanko telegraphed the tsar to tell him on behalf of the duma that only a major political concession on the government's part offered any hope of preserving the imperial power. Nicholas, with that occasional stubbornness that he mistook for decisiveness, ordered the duma to dissolve. It did so formally as an assembly, but an unofficial duma 'Provisional Committee', made up of 12 members, disobeyed the order and remained in session. This marked the first open act of constitutional defiance shown to the tsar. It was immediately followed by the boldest move so far, when Alexander Kerensky, a lawyer and a leading SR member in the duma, called for the tsar to stand down as head of state or be deposed.

On that same day, 27 February, another event took place that was to prove as significant as the refusal of the duma committee to disperse. This was the first meeting of the 'Petrograd Soviet of Soldiers', Sailors' and Workers' Deputies', which gathered in the Tauride Palace, the same building that housed the duma committee. The moving force behind the setting up of the soviet were the Mensheviks, who, under their local leader, Shlyapnikov, had grown in strength in Petrograd during the war.

These two self-appointed bodies – the duma committee, representing the progressive and reformist elements of the old duma, and the soviet, speaking for the striking workers and mutinying soldiers and sailors – became the *de facto* government of Russia. This was the beginning of what became known as the Dual Authority, an uneasy alliance that was to last until October. On 28 February, the soviet published the first edition of its newspaper *Izvestiya* (the News), in which it declared its determination 'to wipe out the old system completely' and to summon a constituent assembly, elected on the basis of universal suffrage.

The remaining ministers in the tsar's cabinet were not prepared to face the growing storm. They used the pretext of an electricity failure in their government offices to abandon their responsibilities and to slip out of the capital. Rodzyanko, who up to this point had struggled to remain loyal to the official government, then advised the tsar that his personal abdication was necessary if the Russian monarchy was to be saved. On 28 February, Nicholas, who appeared to be losing touch with reality, decided to return to Petrograd, apparently in the belief that his personal presence would have a calming effect on the capital. However, the royal train was intercepted on its journey by mutinous troops who forced it to divert to Pskov, a depot 100 miles from Petrograd. A group of generals from the army high command acting together with representatives of the old duma came there to inform the tsar that the situation in Petrograd was so serious as to make his return both futile and dangerous. They, too, advised abdication. Nicholas tamely accepted the advice. His only concern was whether he should also renounce the throne on behalf of his son, Alexei. This he eventually decided to do. The decree of abdication that Nicholas signed on 2 March nominated his brother, the Grand Duke Michael, as the new tsar. However, Michael refused the title on the grounds that it had not been offered to him by a representative Russian constituent Assembly. So it was, in this undramatic way, that the 300-year Romanov dynasty came to an end.

By default the duma committee, which had reconstituted itself as a Provisional Government, thus found itself responsible, with the support of the Petrograd soviet, for governing Russia. On the following day, 3 March, the new government officially informed the rest of the world of the revolution that had taken place.

It is difficult to see the events of 18 February to 3 March as an overthrow of the Russian monarchy. What does stand out in all that went on is the lack of direction and leadership from the top and the unwillingness at the moment of crisis of the tsarist generals and politicians to fight to save the system. Tsardom collapsed from within. The Russian Revolution has often been obscured by later attempts to make it fit into a predetermined pattern of revolutionary change. Marxist historians have seen the events of 1917 as the inevitable triumph of the Bolshevik-led Russian proletariat over their class enemies. This is a controversial viewpoint. Non-Marxists, while generally prepared to accept the significance of the Bolshevik takeover in October 1917, point out that the February Revolution owed almost nothing to Bolshevik influence. Hardly any of the Bolshevik leaders were present in Petrograd, or indeed in Russia, at the time. Stalin and Sverdlov were in distant Siberian exile, Bukharin and Trotsky were in the USA, while Lenin and a group of senior Bolsheviks, including Radek and Zinoviev, were in Switzerland. Indeed, Lenin had been out of Russia for over a decade. With so many of the leading Bolsheviks absent from the country for so long before 1917, and given the difficulties of communication created by the war, their knowledge of the situation in Russia in 1917 was second-hand and fragmentary. It is small wonder, therefore, that the events of February took them by surprise. Strong evidence of this is provided by a statement of Lenin's to a group of students in Zurich in December 1916, only two months before the February Revolution. He told his audience of youthful Bolshevik sympathisers that although they might live to see the proletarian revolution, he did not expect to do so.

One remarkable feature of the Revolution was that it had been overwhelmingly the affair of one city, Petrograd. Another was the willingness of the rest of Russia to accept it. Trotsky observed:

1 It would be no exaggeration to say that Petrograd achieved the February Revolution. The rest of the country adhered to it. There was no struggle anywhere except in Petrograd. There was not to be found anywhere in the country any groups of the
5 population, any parties, institutions, or military units which were ready to put up a fight for the old regime. Neither at the front nor at the rear was there a brigade or regiment prepared to do battle for Nicholas II.

* The February Revolution was not quite the bloodless affair that some of the liberal newspapers claimed. Modern estimates suggest that between 1500 and 2000 people were killed or wounded in the fighting in Petrograd. But by the scale of the casualties regularly suffered by Russian armies in the war this figure was small, further supporting Trotsky's contention that the nation was unwilling to fight to save the old regime.

5 Why the February Revolution Succeeded

It should be emphasised that it was among tsardom's hitherto most committed supporters that the earliest rejection of the tsar occurred. It was the highest-ranking officers who first intimated to Nicholas that he should stand down. It was the aristocratic members of the duma who took the lead in refusing to disband on the tsar's orders. It was when the army and the police told Nicholas that they were unable to carry out his command to keep the populace in order that his position became finally hopeless. The strikes and demonstrations in Petrograd in February 1917 were not so much a cause of the Revolution as a symptom of it. It was the abandonment of the tsar by his traditional supporters at the time of crisis, compounded by Nicholas II's own unwillingness to resist, that brought about revolution and the fall of the Romanov dynasty. Lenin once observed that a true social revolution can occur only when certain preconditions exist; one essential is that the ruling power loses the will to survive. Some time before he formally abdicated, Nicholas had given up the fight. It was not the fact but the speed and completeness of the collapse of tsardom in February 1917 that so took Russian revolutionaries by surprise.

Insofar as a revolution can be spontaneous, the February Revolution was so. It was not an organised affair and it met with little resistance because once the tsar made the decision to go of his own accord there was nothing left to defend. The revolutionaries who hurried back to Petrograd immediately following the collapse of tsardom had not been responsible for that collapse.

   * The character of Tsar Nicholas is important in any analysis of the February Revolution. The evidence suggests that his limited mentality prevented him from ever fully grasping the nature of the events in which he was involved. The Russian poet, Blok, recorded his impression of Nicholas in 1916:

1 Stubborn but without will; nervous but insensitive to everything; distrustful of people, taut and cautious in speech, he was no longer master of the situation, and did not take one clearly conscious step, but gave himself over completely into the hands of
5 those whom he himself had placed in power.

Kerensky similarly described Nicholas as an isolated figure:

1 His mentality and his circumstances kept him wholly out of touch with his people. He heard of the blood and tears of thousands only through official documents, in which they were represented as 'measures' to be taken by the authorities 'in the interests of the
5 peace and safety of the State'. Such reports did not convey to him the pain and and suffering of the victims, but only the 'heroism' of the soldiers, faithful in the fulfilment of their duty to the Tsar and to the Fatherland. From his youth he had been trained to believe that that his welfare and the welfare of Russia were one
10 and the same thing, so that 'disloyal' workmen, peasants and students who were shot down, executed or exiled seemed to him mere monsters who must be destroyed for the sake of the country and the 'faithful subjects' themselves.

The tsar made a number of crucial errors in his handling of the war, the most significant being his decision in 1915 to take direct command of Russia's armed forces. This in effect tied the fate of the Romanov dynasty to the success or otherwise of Russia's armies. There are good grounds for arguing that the war had offered tsardom its last great opportunity to identify itself with the needs of modern Russia and so consolidate itself beyond challenge as the legitimate ruling system. That opportunity was squandered. In 1914 there had been a very genuine enthusiasm for the tsar as representative of the nation. Within three years that enthusiasm had wholly evaporated, even among dedicated tsarists. The fall of Nicholas was the result of weak leadership rather than of savage oppression. He was not helped by his wife's German nationality or by court scandals, of which Rasputin's was the most notorious. But these were minor affairs which by themselves would not have been sufficient to bring down a dynasty.

What destroyed tsardom was the length of the war. A short war, even if unsuccessful, might have been bearable, as Russia's defeat by Japan 12 years earlier had shown. But the cumulative effect of a long-drawn-out struggle proved too destructive to be borne. Deaths and casualties by the million, soaring inflation, a dislocated communications system, hunger and deprivation, all presided over by a series of increasingly bewildered and ineffectual ministries under an incompetent tsar: these were the lot of the Russian people between 1914 and 1917, leading to a loss of morale and a sense of hopelessness that fatally undermined the once-potent myth of the tsar's God-given authority. By 1917 the tsarist system had forfeited all claim to the loyalty of the Russian people.

Making notes on 'War and Revolution 1914–17'

Your aim in studying this chapter should be to gain an understanding of the causes of the February Revolution in 1917. The chapter was so shaped as to give the main sequence of developments from the outbreak of war in 1914 to the abdication of the tsar in 1917. You are recommended to follow this pattern when structuring your own understanding of the connection between war and revolution in Russia.

The following headings and questions should help to direct your thoughts:

1.   Russia's Entry into the First World War
1.1. Why did Russia became involved in war with Germany and Austria?
2.   Russia at War

2.1. The initial surge of support for the tsar
2.2. In what ways were Russia's economic problems deepened by the war?
2.3. Inflation; food shortages; transport
2.4. What was the political effect of Russia's military defeats?
3.   The Growth of Political Opposition
3.1. The recalling of the duma
3.2. What were the aims of the 'The Progressive Bloc'?
3.3. Rasputin's murder
4.   The February Revolution
4.1. Signs of growing unrest
4.2. Open opposition to the tsar in the duma
4.3. Why was the abandonment of the tsar by the officer class so significant?
4.4. In what circumstances was the Petrograd soviet formed?
4.5. What were the terms of Nicholas II's abdication?
5.   Why the February Revolution Succeeded
5.1. The desertion of the tsar's traditional supporters
5.2. How far was Nicholas II responsible for tsardom's collapse?
5.3. What part did the war play in the tsar's downfall?

Answering essay questions on 'War and Revolution 1914–17'

It is an axiom of modern history that a major war puts immense pressures on the nations involved. The war which Russia entered in 1914 had the effect of intensifying all the problems from which she had traditionally suffered. It produced a series of crises which showed up the tsarist system as being politically as well as economically bankrupt. In this context it is worth noting that there is an ongoing debate about whether the war of 1914–17 disrupted Russia's progress towards modernity or whether it merely hastened that irredeemably reactionary country towards its unavoidable revolution. It is important that you are aware of the debate, as it is a very useful vehicle for discussing the essential points relating to the February Revolution. It does not matter which side of the argument you take as long as you can back up your opinion with convincing arguments.

Taking the five main sections of this chapter as listed in the note-making section above, it is possible to pose a number of questions which collectively address the central issues:

1. a) 'Consider the view that in entering the First World War Russia's aims were essentially defensive.'

b) '"Imperial Russia was dragged into the war by the logic of her own mobilisation plans." Discuss.'

2. c) 'How far did Russia's war against Germany and Austria prepare the way for the February Revolution of 1917?'
d) 'To what extent was the breakdown of Russia's transport system responsible for the severity of the conditions in the towns and countryside after 1914?'

3. e) 'Examine the contribution of the duma to the Russian war effort between 1914 and 1917.'
f) 'How appropriate is it to describe the Progressive Bloc as "the last hope of the tsarist system"?'

4. g) '"Not an overthrow from without, but a collapse from within." Consider this verdict on the February Revolution of 1917.'
h) 'Why was so little effort made to save tsardom in February 1917?'

5. i) '"Of all the blunders made by Nicholas II after 1914, his decision to become commander-in-chief of the imperial army proved the most fateful.' Why was this?'
j) 'How important is the character and personality of Nicholas II to an understanding of the reasons for the February Revolution?'

Question 4g is a pivotal one, and if you were to prepare an essay plan for it, it would be a searching test of your grasp of the material covered in the whole chapter.

Do not be deterred by the type of question that requires you to consider a challenging statement, such as the one quoted here. Indeed, rather than being discouraged, you should regard the quotation as a bonus, for what the examiners have done is to provide you with a very direct guide to the response they want from you. Think about how best to interpret the quotation. Be prepared to take time over this; it will be time well spent. In this instance, the quotation could be interpreted more simply as, 'Did tsardom fall or was it pushed?'. What you are being asked is whether Nicholas was toppled by anti-tsarist forces or whether it was his own weakness that obliged him to abdicate. From the notes you have made draw up two lists, one giving the opposition elements, the other containing the tsar's weaknesses. The main part of your answer should consist of these details arranged in such an order as to indicate which were of greater influence in bringing about the February Revolution. An important distinction to be drawn – and you are advised to devote a paragraph to this – is between the tsar's weakness as an individual and the weakness of tsardom as a system of government. It is reasonable to suppose that a stronger individual than Nicholas II as tsar might well have prevented the situation from deteriorating to the point of collapse. Another significant point to stress is that it was the traditional supporters of tsardom, the officer class and the duma, who began the open resistance to the tsar. It was their defection, not the crowds on the streets of Petrograd, that led Nicholas to regard things as hopeless.

Another point that examiners would expect you to make is that the debate on this issue has been considerably influenced by the wish of Bolshevik writers to present 1917 as a proletarian revolution made up of two phases, the first occurring in February. In their view, the overthrow of tsardom was part of the revolutionary process. You do not have to accept or reject this viewpoint, but let the examiner know that you are aware of it and balance it by saying that most disinterested historians emphasise that the absent Bolsheviks played no direct part in the events of February.

Source-based questions on 'War and Revolution 1914–17'

1 Russia enters the war in 1914
Study Sazonov's analysis on page 60, and the French ambassador's description on page 61. Answer the following questions:
a) According to Sazonov, what was the traditional aim of Russian foreign policy towards Turkey and the Balkans? (4 marks)
b) Using your own knowledge and the evidence in the French ambassador's account, explain why Russia's choice between full and partial mobilisation was of such momentous implication in 1914. (5 marks)
c) From your own knowledge and your reading of these sources, would you judge that there is a major difference between the long-term and the immediate causes of Russia's entering the war in 1914? (6 marks)

2 The Causes of the February Revolution
Study Rodzyanko's report on page 65, the British ambassador's description on page 67, and the *Okhrana* agent's report on page 69. Answer the following questions:
a) What light does Rodzyanko's report throw on the state of organisation within the Russian army in 1916? (5 marks)
b) In the light of your own knowledge, assess how appropriately the account of Sturmer's character by the ambassador might be applied as a general description of the quality of the tsar's wartime ministers. (5 marks)
c) How valuable to the historian is the *Okhrana* agent's report as an analysis of the social tensions created by the tsarist government's handling of the war? (5 marks)

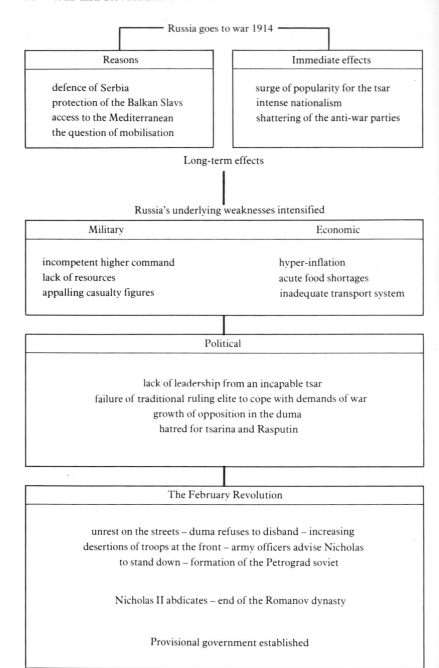

Russia goes to war 1914

Reasons

defence of Serbia
protection of the Balkan Slavs
access to the Mediterranean
the question of mobilisation

Immediate effects

surge of popularity for the tsar
intense nationalism
shattering of the anti-war parties

Long-term effects

Russia's underlying weaknesses intensified

Military

incompetent higher command
lack of resources
appalling casualty figures

Economic

hyper-inflation
acute food shortages
inadequate transport system

Political

lack of leadership from an incapable tsar
failure of traditional ruling elite to cope with demands of war
growth of opposition in the duma
hatred for tsarina and Rasputin

The February Revolution

unrest on the streets – duma refuses to disband – increasing
desertions of troops at the front – army officers advise Nicholas
to stand down – formation of the Petrograd soviet

Nicholas II abdicates – end of the Romanov dynasty

Provisional government established

Summary – War and Revolution 1914–17

3 The role of Nicholas II
Study the descriptions of Nicholas II by Blok and by Kerensky on page
73. Answer the following questions:
a) How closely do Blok and Kerensky agree in their depiction of the
   tsar's character and personality? (4 marks)
b) Using your own knowledge, assess the reliability of these two
   descriptions of Nicholas II. (5 marks)
c) Using your own knowledge and the details in these two sources,
   estimate how far Nicholas II was personally responsible for the
   February Revolution. (6 marks)

CHAPTER 6

1917: The October Revolution

The important point to stress about the Bolshevik Revolution in October 1917 is that it was quite distinct in character and objective from the revolution that had preceded it eight months earlier. The February Revolution had been essentially the collapse of tsardom from within. The October Revolution was a seizure of power by the Bolshevik Party from the Provisional Government, which had replaced the tsar but had proved no more capable of successfully leading Russia in wartime than he had. To understand how this second revolution came about it is necessary to chart the principal developments that occurred in Russia in the period from February to October 1917.

1 The Dual Authority

The Provisional Government, led by Prince Lvov, was the old duma in a new form. When Milyukov, the foreign minister, read out the list of ministers in the newly-formed government someone in the listening crowd called out, 'Who appointed you?'. Milyukov replied, 'We were appointed by the Revolution itself.' In that exchange were expressed the two besetting weaknesses of the Provisional Government as an institution throughout the eight months of its existence. It was not an elected body. It had come into being as a rebellious committee of the old duma, refusing to disband at the tsar's order. As a consequence, it lacked legitimate authority. In the last analysis it was a government by default. It had no constitutional claim upon the loyalty of the Russian people and no natural fund of goodwill on which it could rely. It would be judged entirely on how well it dealt with the nation's problems.

The second major weakness was that the Provisional Government's authority was limited by its unofficial partnership with the Petrograd soviet. It was not that the soviet was initially hostile to the Provisional Government. Indeed, at first, there was a considerable degree of liaison between them. Some individuals were members of both bodies. For example, Alexander Kerensky, the SR leader, was for a time chairman of the soviet as well as a minister in the Provisional Government. The soviet did not set out to be an alternative government. It regarded its role as a watching brief, checking that the interests of the soldiers and workers were fully understood by the new government. However, in the uncertain times that followed the February Revolution, the Provisional Government often seemed unsure of its own authority. Such diffidence tended to emphasise the power-potential of the soviet. There was also the impressive fact that the soviet pattern had spread rapidly and widely in the aftermath of the February Revolution. Soviets soon appeared in all the major cities and towns of Russia. The soviets were to play an increasingly important role in the development of the Revolution, but in the early stages they were not dominated by the Bolsheviks and so were not necessarily opposed to the Provisional Government. It was significant, however, that even before the Bolshevik influence became predominant, the ability of the Petrograd soviet to restrict the Provisional Government's authority had been clearly revealed. In one of its first moves as an organisation it had issued its 'Soviet Order Number 1'. The key clause read:

> The orders of the military commission of the state duma are to be obeyed only in such instances when they do not contradict the orders and decrees of the soviet.

In effect, this document, issued on 2 March and printed in *Pravda* and *Izvestiya*, declared that the orders of the Provisional Government in regard to military affairs were binding only if they were approved by the Petrograd soviet. It is a commonplace of history that any government that cannot directly control its army cannot wield real power. What Order Number 1 made clear was that in post-tsarist Russia the Provisional Government did not have such power. Lacking ultimate control, the government had, therefore, to come to a form of compromise with the soviet. Between February and April this worked as a reasonably effective consensus, which allowed a series of important changes and reforms to take place. A number of factors helped the consensus to survive: one was the general post-revolutionary euphoria experienced in Petrograd in the weeks following the collapse of tsardom. There was a genuine feeling across all the political groups that Russia had entered a period of real freedom. This made co-operation between potentially conflicting parties easier to achieve.

There was also a general acceptance that the new liberty should not be allowed to slip into anarchy, thereby jeopardising the gains of the Revolution. Consequently there was a willingness to maintain an effective form of state authority at the centre of affairs. A further factor was that in their early stages both the Provisional Government and the soviet contained a wider range of political representation than was the case later. Moderate socialists had a bigger influence than the SRs or Bolsheviks in the first meetings of the soviet, while all parties, apart from the Bolsheviks and the monarchists, were represented in the Provisional Government during its early weeks. As the year wore on and the problems mounted, the Provisional Government moved increasingly to the right and the soviet increasingly to the left. But before that shift occurred there had been considerable co-operation.

The fruits of this common approach were shown in such measures as an amnesty for political prisoners, the recognition of trade unions, the introduction of an eight-hour day for industrial workers, the replacement of the tsar's police forces with a 'people's militia', the granting of full civil and religious freedoms, and a commitment to the convening of a constituent assembly. However, those agreed changes did not touch on the critical issues of the war and the land. It would be these that would destroy the always tenuous partnership of the Dual Authority, and it would be Lenin who would begin the process of destruction.

2 Lenin's Return in April

Once the exiled and *émigré* Bolsheviks learned of Nicholas's abdication they rushed back to Petrograd. Those, like Stalin, who had been in Siberia were the first to return in March. Another group with Lenin at their head arrived from Switzerland in April. By the end of that month nearly all the Bolsheviks had returned. Lenin's arrival was a remarkable occurrence both in its manner and its consequences. In the hope that the tsar's fall would be the prelude to the collapse of the Russian armies, the German government arranged for Lenin to return to Russia in a sealed train across German-occupied Europe. The official German pass stated:

1 The carriage will be granted extra-territorial rights. No control or examination of passports or persons may be carried out either on entering or leaving Germany. Persons will be allowed to travel in the carriage absolutely regardless of their political opinions or
5 their attitude towards the question of the desirability of war or peace. As far as possible the journey shall be made without stops and in a through train. The *émigrés* may not be ordered to leave the carriage, nor may they do so on their own initiative. The journey may not be interrupted except in the case of technical
10 necessity.

Lenin's wife, Krupskaya, recorded the event:

1 The moment the news of the February Revolution was received, Ilyich [Lenin] was all eagerness to get back to Russia. As there were no legal ways of travelling, illegal ways would have to be used. But what ways? From the moment the news of the
5 Revolution was received, Ilyich had no sleep. His nights were spent building the most improbable plans. Naturally the Germans gave us permission to travel through Germany in the belief that Revolution was a disaster to a country, and that by allowing emigrant internationalists to return to their country they were
10 helping to spread the Revolution in Russia. The Bolsheviks, for their part, considered it their duty to bring about a victorious proletarian revolution. They did not care what the German bourgeois government thought about it.

* It was the coincidence of German and Bolshevik objectives at this point that made it easy for Lenin's opponents to accuse him of being a German agent, a charge they had continually made against him since the outbreak of war in 1914. The circumstantial evidence appeared to support their accusation. Between 1914 and 1917 the German Foreign Office had given regular financial support to Lenin and the Bolsheviks, in the hope that if they achieved their revolutionary aims they would pull Russia out of the war (see page 107). As Krupskaya observed, Lenin did not really care what the attitude of the Germans was. It just so happened that for quite different reasons what they wanted – the withdrawal of the Russian armies from the war – was precisely what he wanted. However, it made no difference to anti-Bolsheviks that the German reasons were military and Lenin's were political. They considered the German government and the Bolshevik Party to be co-operating in a common cause, the military defeat of Russia.

There is no doubting the great significance of Lenin's return to Petrograd in April 1917. A German official likened it to the transporting of a deadly virus in a test-tube. Once safely arrived in Russia, the test-tube was broken, releasing the fatal germ to infect the body politic of Russia. This was a remarkably apt simile. Up to April 1917 the Petrograd Bolsheviks had accepted the events of February, leading to the formation of the Dual Authority, as part of a genuine revolution. They had been willing to work with the other revolutionary and reformist parties. Lenin changed all that. In his speech on his arrival at Petrograd's Finland Station on 3 April he declared that the February Revolution, far from giving Russia political freedom, had created a 'parliamentary-bourgeois republic'. He condemned the Provisional Government and called for its overthrow in a second revolution. The following day he issued his 'April Theses', in which he spelt out future Bolshevik policy. He defined the events of February not as a genuine class revolution but as a palace *coup* which had simply given authority to ex-tsarist aristocrats and the bourgeoisie. He dismissed the idea of a dual authority. The soviet was the sole body with the right to govern. He rejected the Provisional Government on the grounds that it was the old corrupt, class-ridden, duma in a new garb. For true revolutionaries to accept it or to co-operate with it would be betrayal.

 1 The peculiarity of the current moment in Russia consists in the
   transition from the first stage of the Revolution, which gave
   power to the bourgeoisie as a result of the insufficient conscious-
   ness and organisation of the proletariat, to its second stage, which
 5 should give the power into the hands of the proletariat. The
   present parliamentary-bourgeois republic restricts the independent political life of the masses, hinders their direct participation
   in the democratic upbuilding of the state from the bottom to the
   top. The Soviet of Workers' and Soldiers' Deputies does just the

Lenin speaking in public in Petrograd in 1917. Trotsky is to his left, leaning against the rostrum

10 reverse. What is needed is not a parliamentary republic – a return to that from the Soviet of Workers' Deputies would be a step backwards – but a republic of Soviets throughout the country, growing from below upwards.

Lenin insisted that the Bolsheviks abandon all compromise with other parties and work for the true revolution entirely by their own efforts. The role of the Bolsheviks was not to extend revolutionary freedoms to all classes, but to transfer power to the workers. This was a re-affirmation of his consistent belief that only the Bolshevik Party represented the forces of proletarian revolution. Lenin had ulterior motives in demanding power for the soviets. It was not that he supported them in their present composition and attitude. Indeed, he despised much of what they had done. But the soviets were a power-base. In practice they had become an essential part of the structure of post-tsarist government. Lenin calculated that the soviets – the Petrograd soviet in particular – offered his small Bolshevik Party the means by which they could obtain power in the name of the proletariat. Bolshevik takeover of the soviets would be the prelude to Bolshevik takeover of the state.

The essence of Lenin's argument was summed up in a set of provocative slogans: 'Peace, Bread and Land' and 'All Power to the Soviets'. These proved to be more than slogans; they encapsulated the basic problems confronting Russia. It was the Provisional Government's incapacity in the face of these difficulties that was to bring about its collapse.

3 The Provisional Government

The position of the Provisional Government was precarious from the first. To its structural and constitutional difficulties were added the outstanding problems identified by Lenin in the April Theses: the war with Germany, the chronic food shortage, and the disruption in the countryside.

The dominant problem was the war. For the Provisional Government after February 1917 there was no choice but to continue to fight. It was the essential condition of its receiving supplies and war-credits from the western allies. Tsardom had left Russia virtually bankrupt. No government could have carried on without large injections of capital from abroad, and the foreign bankers were among the first to visit Russia after Nicholas's abdication to ensure that the new regime was committed to pursuing the war. The strain that this military obligation imposed on the Provisional Government proved ultimately to be unsustainable. Its preoccupation with the war destroyed any possibility that the government would deal adequately with Russia's social and economic problems. The Provisional Government was thus from the beginning in an impossible and paradoxical situation: in order to survive it had to keep Russia in the war, but in keeping Russia in the war it destroyed its chances of survival.

By 1917 the people who did the actual fighting – the soldiers – had overwhelmingly lost the will to continue. The attempt by the government to rekindle the patriotic enthusiasm of 1914 met with very limited response. In contrast, the Bolshevik agitators, who encouraged mutiny and desertion in the armed services by describing the futility of the war, found ready listeners among the troops at the front and the reservists waiting to be sent there.

* The question of the war brought about the first serious disagreement between the Petrograd soviet and the Provisional Government. On 14 March the soviet had issued an 'Address to the people of the whole world, declaring for peace without annexations or indemnities'. Nonsense was made of the government's declared acceptance of the 'Address' by the repeated assurances of Milyukov, the foreign minister, that Russia would continue to play her full military role as one of the allies. Late in April, a series of violent demonstrations occurred in Petrograd directed against Milyukov. These resulted in a crisis within the government. Milyukov and Guchkov, the war minister, resigned

early in May. These resignations were an illustration of the divisions within the government as well as of the outside pressures on it. In the reshuffled cabinet, Kerensky become the war minister and places were found for the leading Mensheviks and SRs. It was hoped that this apparent leftward shift of the Provisional Government would strengthen it through its closer ties with the soviet. In fact, the opposite happened. The socialists in the government tended to become isolated from the soviet. This was because in joining the government they had necessarily to enter into coalition with the Kadets. This laid them open to the charge that they were compromising with the bourgeoisie. Lenin wrote of 'those despicable socialists who have sold out to the Government'.

Some individuals within the Provisional Government may have had misgivings about continuing the war, but at no time did the government as a body contemplate abandoning its military commitment. This would not have mattered had the Russian armies been at all successful, but the military situation continued to deteriorate, eroding such support as the government had initially enjoyed. Lvov stayed as nominal head of the government but it was Kerensky who increasingly became the major influence. As war minister, he took the line that Russia should view the conflict with Germany as a struggle to save the Revolution, requiring the total dedication of the nation. He made a number of personal visits to the front to deliver passionate speeches to the troops. He later described his efforts:

For the sake of the nation's life it was necessary to restore the army's will to die. 'Forward to the battle for freedom. I summon you not to a feast but death.' These were the words I used before the troops in the frontline positions.

This attempt to turn the war into a revolutionary crusade took no account of the real situation. The fact was that Russia had gone beyond the point where she could fight a successful war. Yet Kerensky persisted. In June, a major offensive was launched against the Austro-German armies on the south-western front. It failed badly. With their already low morale further weakened by Bolshevik subversion, the Russian forces were no match for the Germans, who easily repulsed them and inflicted heavy losses. Whole regiments mutinied or deserted. General Kornilov, the commander on the south-western front, called on the Provisional Government to halt the offensive and to direct its energies into crushing the political subversives by the most rigorous means. This appeal for a tougher policy was taken up by the government. Lvov stood down as prime minister, being replaced by Kerensky. Kornilov became commander-in-chief.

The government's troubles were deepened by events on the island of Kronstadt, the naval base situated 15 miles west of Petrograd in the Bay of Finland. Sailors and workers there defied the central authorities by setting up their own separate government. Such developments tempted a number of revolutionaries in Petrograd into thinking that the time and opportunity had come for them to bring down the Provisional Government. The events surrounding the attempt to do so became known as 'The July Days'.

a) The July Days

By the summer of 1917 it did, indeed, seem that the government's authority was irreparably breaking down. The spread of soviets, the growth of trade unions, worker-control of the factories, the widespread seizure of land by the peasants and the creation of independent national minority governments – most notably in the Ukraine – suggested that the Provisional Government could no longer control events. It was the Ukrainian question that helped to provoke the July Days crisis. When the Kadet ministers in the coalition learned in late June that a Provisional Government deputation in Kiev had offered autonomy to the Ukraine, they resigned, protesting that only a constituent assembly could properly decide such matters. This ministerial crisis coincided with large-scale street demonstrations in Petrograd. Demonstrations were not uncommon; they had been almost a daily occurrence since February. But in the atmosphere created by the news of the failure of the south-western offensive and the government's mounting problems the protests of early July turned into a direct challenge to the Provisional Government.

There was much confusion and it is not entirely clear who initiated the rising of 3–6 July. A month earlier at the first All-Russian Congress of Soviets, Lenin had declared that the Bolshevik Party was ready to take power, but the delegates had regarded this as rhetoric rather than an immediate intention. It is also true that there were SRs and other non-Bolshevik revolutionaries in the soviet who for some time had been demanding that the Petrograd soviet supersede the Provisional Government. Trotsky later referred to the July Days as a 'semi-insurrection' and argued that it had been begun by the Mensheviks and SRs. In saying this, he was trying to absolve the Bolsheviks from the blame of having started a rising that failed. The explanation offered afterwards by the Bolsheviks was that they had come heroically to the aid of the workers of Petrograd and their comrades-in-arms, the sailors of Kronstadt, who had risen spontaneously against the government. The opposite point of view was put at the time by Chkheidze, the Menshevik chairman of the soviet. He asserted that the Bolsheviks, having been behind the rising from the beginning, later tried to disclaim responsibility.

* The rising itself was a confused, disorderly affair. In the course of the three days the demonstrators fell out amongst themselves, often

physically attacking those members of the soviet who seemed reluctant to make a real bid for power. In such circumstances it was relatively easy for the Provisional Government to crush the rising. Troops loyal to the government were rushed from the front. They duly scattered the demonstrators and restored order.

While the origins of the July Days may have been uncertain, the results were not. The unsuccessful rising clearly revealed a number of important facts: that the opposition forces were disunited in their aims and methods, that the Bolsheviks were still far from being the dominant revolutionary party, and that the Provisional Government still retained enough of its residual authority to be able to put down an armed insurrection. This last revelation did much to raise the spirits of the Provisional Government and brought particular credit to Kerensky as war minister. Two days after the rising had been crushed he became prime minister.

Whatever the Bolshevik responsibility for the July Days, Kerensky now seized the opportunity provided by their failure to renew his efforts to suppress, if not destroy, the Bolshevik Party. *Pravda* was closed down, many of the Bolshevik leaders including Trotsky and Kamenev were arrested, and Lenin was forced to flee to Finland. Kerensky also launched a propaganda campaign in which Lenin and his party were branded as traitors and agents in the pay of the German high command. A fortnight after the July Days, the Bolshevik Party stood on the verge of destruction as a political force in Russia.

b) The Land Question

That the Bolsheviks survived was largely due to the errors at critical moments of the Provisional Government. Just as the government misread the public attitude towards the war, so, too, it failed to appreciate the prevailing view of the land question. Land-shortage was a chronic social problem in Russia; it had been a chief cause of peasant unrest since the emancipation of the serfs in 1861. The February Revolution had led the peasantry to believe that they would be the beneficiaries of a major land redistribution. They had expected that the estates of the landlords and the Church would be appropriated and given to them. When this did not happen, the peasants in many parts of Russia took the law into their own hands and seized the property and estates of local landlords. Disturbances in the countryside occurred daily throughout 1917. It would not be an exaggeration to describe this as a national peasants' revolt.

Neither the Provisional Government nor the Bolshevik Party had a real answer to the land problem or a genuine policy towards the peasantry. The Provisional Government had set up a Land Commission with the avowed object of redistributing land, but this body made little headway in handling a massive administrative task. It was doubtful,

A clean-shaven and bewigged Lenin in hiding in 1917

moreover, whether the government's heart was ever really in land reform. The majority of its members came, after all, from the landed and propertied classes. They were unlikely to be enthusiasts for a policy that would threaten their own social position. They had supported the February Revolution as a political change but not as a social upheaval. They were quite willing to see the estates of the fallen monarchy used to satisfy the peasants' craving for land, but they had no intention of losing their own possessions in a general redistribution of property. This had been the thrust of Lenin's assertion in the 'April Theses' that tsardom had been replaced not by a revolutionary but by a bourgeois regime.

★ Yet there was a sense in which the land issue was equally difficult for the Bolsheviks. As a Marxist party, they had dismissed the peasantry as, in Trotsky's words, 'the pack animal' of history, lacking true revolutionary initiative. By definition the proletarian revolution was an affair of the industrial working class. Lenin, on his return in April, had declared: 'It is not possible for a proletarian party to rest its hopes at this time on a community of interest with the peasantry'. However, faced with the continuation of peasant land-seizures throughout Russia, Lenin was quite prepared to make a tactical adjustment. Appreciating that it was impossible to ignore the disruptive behaviour of four-fifths of the Russian population, he asserted that the special circumstances of post-tsarist Russia had produced a situation in which for the last time in their history the peasants were acting as a truly revolutionary force. This modification of Marxist theory thus allowed Lenin to add the Russian peasants to the proletarian cause. He calculated that since the bulk of the Russian soldiers were peasants in uniform, wearied with the war and yearning to be home, they were likely to be attracted by his anti-war policy.

Lenin, at first, had no specific land policy to offer. Given its original disregard of the peasant question, the Bolshevik Party had not bothered to produce one. So, he did the next best thing. He simply took over the land policy of the Social Revolutionaries, the peasant party, using their slogans and often copying their statements word for word. 'Land to the Peasants' became the new Bolshevik catchphrase. What this meant in mid-1917 was that the Bolsheviks recognised the peasant land-seizures as a *fait accompli*. Lenin declared that what the peasantry had done was wholly in keeping with 'revolutionary legality' and therefore irreversible. This acceptance of the peasant position produced a considerable swing to the Bolsheviks in the countryside. It had the further effect of splitting the SRs, a significant number of whom began to align themselves with the Bolsheviks. Known as Left SRs, they sided with the Bolshevik Party on all major issues.

c) The Kornilov Affair

In August, the Provisional Government became involved in the Kornilov Affair, a crisis that both took away the gains it had made from its handling of the July Days and allowed the Bolsheviks to recover from their humiliation. Parts of the story have been obscured by the conflicting descriptions given later by some of the leading participants, but there was little doubt as to the intentions of the chief figure in the episode, General Kornilov, the new commander-in-chief. Kornilov was a representative of the type of right-wing army officer who had never accepted the February Revolution. He believed that before Russia could fulfil her patriotic duty to defeat Germany, her first need was to bring about internal stability by destroying the socialist enemies within. 'It's time to hang the German supporters and spies, with Lenin at their head, and to disperse the Soviet.'

By late August, the advance of German forces deeper into Russia began to threaten Petrograd itself. Large numbers of refugees and deserters flocked into the city, heightening the tension there and creating serious disorder. Kornilov declared that Russia was about to topple into anarchy and that the government stood in grave danger of a socialist-inspired insurrection. He informed Kerensky that he intended to bring his loyal troops to Petrograd to save the Provisional Government from being overthrown.

Accounts tend to diverge at this point in their description of Kerensky's response. Those who believe that he was involved in a plot with Kornilov to destroy the soviet and set up a dictatorship argue that Kerensky had at first fully supported this move, and that it was only subsequently, when he realised that Kornilov was intent on removing the Provisional Government as well and establishing military rule, that he turned against him. Other commentators, sympathetic to Kerensky, maintain that he had not colluded with Kornilov and that his actions had been wholly consistent. They also point to the fact that a special Commission of Enquiry into the affair in 1917 cleared Kerensky of any complicity. But however the question of collusion is decided, it was certainly the case that Kerensky publicly condemned Kornilov's advance. He ordered him to surrender his post and placed Petrograd under martial law. Kornilov reacted to this by sending an open telegram, declaring:

1 People of Russia! Our great motherland is dying. I, General Kornilov declare that under pressure of the Bolshevik majority in the soviets, the Provisional Government is acting in complete accord with the plans of the German General Staff. It is des-
5 troying the army and is undermining the very foundations of the country.

Fearful that Kornilov would attack, Kerensky called on all loyal citizens to take up arms to defend the city. The Bolsheviks were released from prison or came out of hiding to collect the weapons issued by the Provisional Government to all who were willing to fight. By this strange twist in the story of 1917, the Bolsheviks found themselves being given arms by the very government they were pledged to overthrow. As it happened, the weapons were not needed against Kornilov. The railway workers refused to operate the trains to bring Kornilov's army to Petrograd. Faced with such obstruction and dismayed by the news of the formation of a mass workers' militia ready to oppose him, Kornilov abandoned his advance and allowed himself to be arrested.

Despite the obvious readiness of the people of Petrograd to resist a military takeover, the Kornilov episode did not strengthen the Provisional Government's position or that of Kerensky. He later admitted regretfully that the affair had been 'the prelude to the October Revolution'. It had further exposed the political weakness of the Provisional Government and had shown how vulnerable it was in the face of military threat. Lenin was now convinced that the government was 'ripe for plucking'. Certainly it was the Bolsheviks who gained most from the failure of Kornilov's attempted *coup*. They had been able to present themselves as defenders of Petrograd and the Revolution, thus wiping out the memories of the debacle of the July Days.

4 The October Revolution

The measure of the Bolsheviks' recovery was soon apparent. By the middle of September they had gained a majority in both the Petrograd and Moscow soviets. However, this should not be seen as indicating a large swing of opinion in their favour, but rather as a reflection of the changing character of the soviets. In the first few months after the February Revolution the meetings of the soviets had been fully attended. Over 3000 deputies had packed into the gatherings of the Petrograd soviet at the Tauride Palace. But as the months passed, enthusiasm had waned. By the autumn of 1917 attendance was often down to a few hundred. This was a great advantage to the Bolsheviks. Their political dedication meant that they continued to turn up in force while the members of the other parties attended irregularly. The result was that the Bolshevik Party exerted an influence out of proportion to its numbers. This was especially the case in regard to the composition of the various sub-committees.

Broadly what happened in Petrograd following the Kornilov Affair was that the soviet moved to the left while the Provisional Government shifted to the right. This made some form of clash between the two bodies increasingly likely. Lenin put it as a matter of stark choice: 'Either a soviet government or Kornilovism. There is no middle course'. From his exile in Finland, Lenin constantly urged his party to prepare for the immediate overthrow of Kerensky's government. He claimed that his earlier estimate of what would happen had proved wholly correct: that the Provisional Government, incapable of solving the war and land questions, would become increasingly counter-revolutionary while the soviet would become the only hope of true revolutionaries. He further argued that the Bolsheviks could not wait; they must seize the moment while the government was at its most vulnerable. In a sentence that was to become part of Bolshevik folklore, Lenin wrote on 12 September: 'History will not forgive us if we do not assume power'.

Lenin's sense of urgency derived from his anxiety in regard to two events, scheduled to take place in the autumn, which he calculated would seriously limit the Bolsheviks' future freedom of action. One was the meeting of the All-Russian Congress of Soviets in late October; the other was the November election for the Constituent Assembly. His conviction was that the Bolsheviks would have to take power before these events occurred. If the Bolsheviks, under the banner 'All Power to the Soviets', could topple the Provisional Government before the congress met they could then present their new authority as a *fait accompli* which the congress would have no reason to reject. The Constituent Assembly elections presented a somewhat different problem. This was the body on which all progressives and reformers had set their hopes. Once it came into being its moral authority would be difficult to challenge. Lenin told his party that since it was hard to judge how well the Bolsheviks would fare in the elections, they would have to be in power before the results were announced. This would provide them with the authority to undermine the results should they prove unfavourable.

* At the same time as Lenin pressed this policy upon the Bolsheviks, Kerensky, in an effort to make his government's position less vulnerable, again reshuffled the cabinet and announced plans for a 'Pre-Parliament', a body intended to fill the interim before the Constituent Assembly came into being. Lenin condemned the Pre-Parliament as a manoeuvre to strengthen the bourgeoisie's grip on the government. Acting on his orders, the Bolshevik members of the soviet who were entitled to attend the Pre-Parliament first derided it and then walked out.

Despite the power with which Lenin put his arguments to his colleagues, there were Bolsheviks on the Central Committee of the party who doubted the wisdom of striking against the Provisional Government at this point. In an effort to enforce conformity, Lenin slipped back into Petrograd on 7 October. His personal presence stiffened Bolshevik resolve, but did not produce total unity. During the next two weeks he spent exhausting hours at a series of Central Committee meetings trying to persuade the waverers to abandon their caution. On 10 October, the Central Committee pledged itself in principle to an armed insurrection, but could not agree on a specific date. In the end, by another quirk of fate, it was Kerensky and the government, not the Bolsheviks, who initiated the actual rising.

Rumours of an imminent Bolshevik *coup* had been circulating for some weeks, but it was not until an article, written by two members of the Bolshevik Central Committee, appeared in a revolutionary journal that the authorities felt they had sure proof. In the article, the writers, Zinoviev and Kamenev, argued strongly that it would be a mistake to attempt to overthrow the government at that point. Kerensky interpreted the article as indicating that a date had been set. Rather than wait to be caught off guard, he ordered a pre-emptive attack on the Bolsheviks. On 23 October, the Bolshevik newspapers, *Pravda* and *Izvestiya*, were closed down by government troops and an attempted round-up of the leading Bolsheviks began. The Bolsheviks no longer had a choice; Lenin ordered the planned insurrection to begin.

That there was a plan at all was due not to Lenin, but to Trotsky. While it was Lenin who was undoubtedly the great influence behind the October Rising, it was Trotsky who actually organised it. The key to Trotsky's success in this was his chairmanship of the Petrograd soviet, to which he had been elected in September. As the dominant member of the three-man Military Revolutionary Committee (MRC) of the soviet, it was Trotsky who had drafted the plans for the overthrow of the Provisional Government. When Lenin gave the order for the uprising to begin, it was Trotsky who directed the Red Guards in their seizure of the key installations and vantage points in Petrograd.

* In the three days (25–27 October) that it took for the city to fall under Bolshevik control there was remarkably little fighting. There appears to have been no more than five fatalities during the whole episode. The simple fact was that the Provisional Government had hardly any military resources on which it could call. Desertions had reduced the Petrograd garrison to a few loyal officer-cadets, a small group of cossacks, and a battalion of women soldiers (known as the 'Amazons') whom Kerensky had specially recruited earlier in the year as an example of the fighting spirit of the Russian people. Faced by the Red Guards, the cossacks deserted, while the cadets and the Amazons were persuaded that an attempt to resist would be futile. When the Red Guards approached the Winter Palace (the headquarters of the Provisional Government), they met with minimal resistance. The sounding of its guns by the cruiser *Aurora*, moored in the River Neva, whose crew had declared their support for the soviet, convinced the remaining members of the government that their position was hopeless. As many as were able escaped unnoticed out of the building. Kerensky himself, having earlier left the city in a vain effort to raise loyal troops, fled to the American embassy and subsequently to the USA.

On the night of 27 October, Lenin informed the somewhat bewildered delegates to the Congress of Soviets, who had begun their first session that evening, that the Bolshevik-led Petrograd soviet had seized power in their name. He then proceeded to read out the list of commissars (ministers) of the new revolutionary government (*Sovnarkom*). His own name was at the head as chairman. The right-wing SRs and the Mensheviks walked out, protesting that it had been a Bolshevik *coup*, not a soviet assumption of power. Trotsky jeered after them that they and their kind had 'consigned themselves to the dustbin of history'. Lenin then announced to the Bolsheviks and the SRs who remained that they would now proceed 'to construct the towering edifice of socialist society'.

The failure of the Provisional Government to rally effective military support in its hour of need was symptomatic of its much deeper political failure over the previous eight months. It was not that the Provisional Government was bitterly rejected by the Russian people. It

Kerensky's Amazons

was more a matter of its basic inability to arouse genuine enthusiasm. Kerensky's government had come nowhere near to solving Russia's problems or satisfying her needs. Hence its support had evaporated. Politically inept, economically incompetent and militarily disastrous, the Provisional Government was not considered to be worth struggling to save. In October 1917 the Bolsheviks were pushing against an already open door.

5 Reasons for Bolshevik Success

Trotsky later ascribed the success of the Bolshevik rising to three factors: 'the refusal of the Petrograd garrison to side with the government, the creation of the MRC, and the infiltration by Bolshevik commissars of the key divisions of the army'. These, he wrote, 'completely isolated not only the general staff of the Petrograd zone, but also the government'.

The question arises as to why none of the other parties was able to mount a serious challenge to the Bolsheviks for the leadership of the Revolution between February and October. One answer is that they had all accepted February as a genuine revolution. Consequently it made sense for them to co-operate with the Provisional Government, which claimed to represent a cross-section of the progressive forces in Russia. The result was that the supposedly revolutionary parties were prepared to enter into coalition with the Kadets, the dominant party in the government, and await the convening of the Constituent Assembly. This gave the Bolsheviks a powerful propaganda weapon. Lenin made great play of the socialists' having sold out to the bourgeoisie.

Another explanation is that the other parties were weakened by their support for the war. None of them opposed the continuation of the struggle against Germany with the consistency that Lenin's Bolsheviks did after April 1917. The non-Bolshevik parties regarded it as Russia's duty to defeat the enemy. The SRs, the Mensheviks and, indeed, some individual Bolsheviks believed wholeheartedly in a revolutionary war against bourgeois Germany. On the left of the Menshevik Party there was a vociferous wing of international revolutionaries who saw the war as the ideal opportunity for beginning the worldwide class struggle. Moreover, as committed Marxists, the Mensheviks had every reason for co-operating with the Provisional Government rather than opposing it. They saw the February Revolution as marking a critical stage in the class war, when the bourgeoisie had overthrown the old feudal forces represented by the tsar. This stage, as Marx had argued, was the necessary prelude to the revolution of the proletariat. However, the Mensheviks judged that since Russia did not yet possess a proletariat large enough to be a truly revolutionary force, it was their immediate task to align themselves with the other parties in a broad front to work for the consolidation of the bourgeois revolution before turning to the ultimate objective of the proletarian rising. One of the interesting paradoxes of the Russian Revolution is that, in strictly theoretical terms, the Mensheviks were always more consistent in their Marxism that were Lenin and his Bolsheviks.

* In this context it is important to remember the lack of a tradition of party politics in tsarist Russia. With the fall of tsardom, the various parties found themselves for a brief, heady, period free to advance their views, but there were no accepted rules of political conduct which they could follow. The arts of compromise, of give-and-take, and of negotiation, which had developed in western Europe were unknown in Russia. In their absence, politics was reduced to a simple question of who could gain power and then assert it over others. Lenin expressed it in the simple formulation: 'who, whom?' Democracy did not enter into it. Power would go to the most flexible and the most ruthless party. The Bolsheviks under Lenin were perfectly suited to exploit the situation. Whatever adjustments circumstances required them to make, they never lost sight of their basic goal – the seizure of power. This did not make their position unassailable – the near-fiasco of the July Days had disproved that; nor that their takeover in October was inevitable – that depended as much on the weakness and mistakes of their opponents as upon their own resolution. But it did mean that none of the contending parties was as well equipped as the Bolsheviks to exploit the crises facing Russia in 1917.

Tseretelli, a Menshevik and a leading member of the Petrograd soviet before its domination by the Bolsheviks, admitted: 'Everything we did at that time was a vain effort to hold back a destructive elemental flood with a handful of insignificant chips'. Struve, a liberal *émigré*, observed: 'Only Bolshevism was logical about revolution and true to its essence, and therefore in the revolution it conquered'. Milyukov, the Kadet leader, shared Struve's view of the Bolsheviks: 'They knew where they were going, and they went in the direction which they had chosen once and for all toward a goal which came nearer with every new, unsuccessful, experiment of compromise'.

* In assessing the reasons why the Provisional Government did not survive, it should be emphasised that it had never been meant to last. As its very title suggested, it was intended to be an interim government. Along with its partner in the Dual Authority, the Petrograd soviet, its role was to provide a caretaker administration until an all-Russian Constituent Assembly could be elected in the autumn. The Constituent Assembly was the ultimate dream of all liberals and democrats; it would be the first fully-elected, nationwide, democratic parliament in Russia. All parties, including the Bolsheviks, were committed to the Assembly. As a consequence, the Provisional Government was always open to the charge that as an unelected, self-appointed body, it had no right to exercise the authority that could properly belong only to the Constituent Assembly. Such limited strength as the Provisional Government

had came from its claim to be the representative of the February Revolution. Lenin made it his task to undermine that claim.

One of the ironies of the situation was that both the Provisional Government and the Bolsheviks overestimated each other's strength, each delaying their moves against the other for fear of overplaying their hand. Historians have often wondered why the Provisional Government did not make a more sustained effort to destroy the Bolsheviks politically. It is true that some arrests were made, but the government's efforts at suppression were half-hearted and desultory. Sukhanov, a Menshevik eye-witness of the events of 1917, calculated that so limited was the Bolshevik military strength at the time of the October Rising that 'a good detachment of 500 men would have been enough to liquidate Smolny [the Bolshevik headquarters] and everybody in it'. Trotsky agreed, but asked derisively where the Provisional Government was to get 500 good men to support it. For their part, the Bolsheviks miscalculated the strength and effectiveness of the Provisional Government. Lenin expected to be summarily shot if ever the government's agents found him. Believing himself to be a prime target, he spent the greater part of his time between April and October in disguise in a variety of hide-outs. It says much for the power of Lenin's personality and reputation that he continued to exercise a decisive influence over the actions of the Bolshevik Party during these critical months when he was either incognito or absent altogether from Petrograd.

It is important not to overestimate Lenin's power to dictate events in 1917. In the standard Bolshevik version of what happened, Lenin was portrayed as having fulfilled his plans for revolution along the lines he had laid down in such writings as his 1902 pamphlet, *What Is To Be Done?* This had visualised the development of a tightly-knit, disciplined Bolshevik Party which would seize power in the name of the masses at the opportune moment. Modern researchers, while accepting the importance of Lenin's role in the Revolution, point out that the structure and authority of his party in 1917 were significantly different from his 1902 model. The evidence of the many disputes within Bolshevik ranks over policy between February and October suggests that they were by no means as disciplined or centrally-controlled as Lenin would have wished. Part of the explanation for this is that the composition of the party had changed in ways which Lenin and the Central Committee had not planned. After the February Revolution there had been a major increase in membership which the Central Committee had not wanted but which, in the mixture of post-Revolution enthusiasm and political confusion, they seemed unable to prevent. The following figures, calculated by Western analysts, are tentative, but they do indicate the remarkable transformation which the Bolshevik Party underwent in 1917:

Number of members in 1917

February: 25,000   April: 100,000   October: 340,000
                                             (60,000 in Petrograd)

Modern historians view this influx of party members as an aspect of the general radicalisation of Russian politics that occurred as the Provisional Government showed itself to be increasingly incapable of dealing with the problems confronting the nation. What had helped to prepare the ground for the successful Bolshevik *coup* in October was the growth in the Petrograd factories of workers' committees which, while not necessarily pro-Bolshevik, were certainly not pro-government. One result of the anti-government agitation of these committees was that, when the open challenge to the Provisional Government came in October, Kerensky's desperate appeal for support from the people of Petrograd went unheeded.

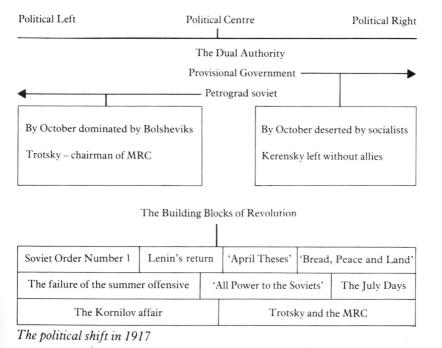

The political shift in 1917

Making notes on '1917: The October Revolution'

This chapter attempts to explain the October Revolution by reference to the key developments between February and October 1917. Those months were a period of rapid and often dramatic change. Since effective analysis depends on sound chronology, it is important when studying 1917 to acquire an understanding of the order in which events occurred. The following headings should help you to do this.

1.   The Dual Authority
1.1. The origins and composition of the Provisional Government and the Petrograd soviet
2.   Lenin's Return in April
2.1. The manner of his return
2.2. Lenin's 'April Theses'
3.   The Provisional Government
3.1. How did the Provisional Government's policy towards the war weaken its position?
3.2. The causes and effects of the July Days
3.3. Why did neither the Provisional Government nor the Bolsheviks have a genuine land policy?
3.4. The impact of the Kornilov affair
4.   The October Revolution
4.1. Why did the Provisional Government and the soviet increasingly draw apart?
4.2. Lenin's sense of urgency
4.3. The 'Pre-Parliament'
4.4. What prompted Kerensky's pre-emptive strike?
4.5. What was Trotsky's role in the preparation of a Bolshevik rising?
4.6. The October coup
5.   Reasons for Bolshevik success
5.1. The weakness of the non-Bolshevik parties
5.2. Lenin's contribution
5.3. What were the main weaknesses of the Provisional Government?
5.4. The character of Bolshevism

Answering essay questions on '1917: The October Revolution'

As you might judge from the importance of the topic, the October Revolution of 1917 is a rich vein from which questions are mined. There is one question that could be said to cover everything of importance: 'Why did the Provisional Government fail and the Bolshevik Party succeed in 1917?'. However, precisely because it does cover practically everything it is highly unlikely that it would ever be set as a single question. What needs to be done, therefore, is to frame a range of questions that each contribute to building an effective response to the larger question. Three main lines of approach may be suggested (with sub-points in accordance with the list of notes above). These, while not touching on every possible question, do cover the essentials.

A. *The Provisional Government and its problems* – its uncertain status – its relations with the Petrograd soviet in the Dual Authority – the war question – the land and food problem – the July Days – the Kornilov affair.

B. *Lenin and the Bolsheviks* – the 'April Theses' – 'Peace, Bread and land' – 'All Power to the Soviets' – the July Days – the October Rising.

C. *The October Revolution* – Bolshevik preparations – Provisional Government weakness – the rising itself – reasons for government collapse and Bolshevik success.

There is obviously considerable overlap and common ground between these themes and their sub-sections. The Dual Authority is a very useful central strand, connecting the status and power of the government and the Petrograd soviet, the 'April Theses', the Bolshevik policy of 'All Power to the Soviets', and the final collapse of Kerensky's government.

Questions on these central themes might include:

A. 1. '"The Provisional Government was doomed to failure because from the first its authority was nominal rather than real." Discuss.'
   2. 'Consider the view that the Bolshevik slogans, "Bread, Peace and Land" were accurate definitions of the basic problems confronting the Provisional Government.'
B. 3. 'Estimate the significance of Lenin's return to Russia in April.'
   4. 'How was it that only three months after their failure in the July Days the Bolsheviks were in a position to take power?'
C. 5. 'Why was there so little resistance to the Bolshevik seizure of power in October 1917?'
   6. '"A revolution played by notes": consider this view of the October Rising.'

A possible approach to question 4 would be:

(1) Begin with a list of the principal developments between July and October. These should include such points as the July Days, the Kornilov affair, the increasing desertions from the front, the growing disillusionment with and within the Provisional Government regarding its failure to solve Russia's outstanding problems, and the increasing

Bolshevik influence in the Petrograd soviet. *(2)* From this list you can then fashion the features of the main points of the answer. An appropriate opening would be to explain that the Bolsheviks recovered from the July Days debacle largely because the Provisional Government seemed disinclined to press home their political advantage over them. Moreover, whatever advantage the government had held was lost when the Bolsheviks were able to pose as defenders of Petrograd and the Revolution against Kornilov. *(3)* The main body of the answer should emphasise how the authority of the Provisional Government, which had always been conditional on its being able to meet the challenges facing Russia, was steadily eroded by the Petrograd soviet, in which the Bolsheviks became increasingly influential. *(4)* It would be worth stressing that the question of Bolshevik recovery cannot be considered in isolation. Indeed, it is arguable that Provisional Government decline was more significant than rising Bolshevik strength. *(5)* In this context, attention should be drawn to the misjudgement by Kerensky's government of the strength of Lenin's party. In fact, each side over-estimated the power of the other and tended to play a waiting game, fearful of exposing its own weakness. Although Trotsky's plans for a *coup* against the government had been drawn up for some time, in the event the rising was occasioned by Kerensky's attempt at a pre-emptive strike against the Bolsheviks. *(6)* Trotsky's key role as chairman of the soviet's MRC was vitally important since, in fulfilment of Lenin's long-standing aim, it enabled the Bolsheviks to dress their objectives in a soviet cloak. *(7)* In the concluding part of the answer stress should be laid on the inability of the Provisional Government either to conduct a successful war or withdraw from it. This, together with its poor record with regard to the issues of 'bread and land', encouraged a drift to the left in Russian politics. When the challenge came in October, the Provisional Government found itself without allies. The Bolsheviks did not so much seize power as pick it up after it had been dropped. A useful quotation with which to end the essay might be: 'the Bolsheviks did not inherit a ship of state, they took over a derelict hulk'.

Source-based questions on '1917: The October Revolution'

1 Lenin's return in April
Read the extracts from the German pass and from Krupskaya's account on page 82. Answer the following questions:
a) Explain the following phrases:
   'extra-territorial rights' (page 82, line 1) (2 marks)
   'emigrant internationalists' (page 82, line 9). (2 marks)
b) How far do the official pass and Krupskaya's account agree in their

depiction of German attitudes towards Lenin in April 1917? (6 marks)

c) Using your own knowledge and the evidence in these two sources, examine how far Lenin's objectives in returning to Russia in April 1917 were subsequently fulfilled. (9 marks)

2 The Provisional Government

Read the extracts from the 'Soviet Order Number 1' (page 81), from Kerensky's appeal (page 86, and from Kornilov's telegram (page 91). Answer the following questions:

a) Explain the implications for the Provisional Government of 'Soviet Order Number 1.' (3 marks)

b) In what respects does Kerensky's statement on page 86 indicate the predicament of the Provisional Government in regard to the continuation of the war against Germany? (4 marks)

c) Using your own knowledge, comment on the accuracy of Kornilov's assertion 'under pressure of the Bolshevik majority in the soviets, the Provisional Government is acting in complete accord with . . . the German General Staff' (page 91 line 2). (4 marks)

d) In what ways do these three sources illustrate the basic difficulties under which the Provisional Government laboured during its period of office? Quote brief extracts to substantiate your points. (8 marks)

3 The October Revolution

Read Lenin's analysis on page 83, and Trotsky's on page 96. Answer the following questions:

a) Using only the evidence in the source on page 83, explain why Lenin regarded a second revolution as being necessary in 1917. (4 marks)

b) How far do Lenin and Trotsky, as represented in these two extracts, agree in their analysis of the revolutionary situation in Russia in 1917? (6 marks)

c) In the light of your own knowledge, assess how closely the Bolshevik takeover in October conformed to the ideas of revolution as defined by Lenin in the extract on page 83. (9 marks)

CHAPTER 7

The Bolshevik Consolidation of Power 1918–21

As many historians have pointed out, the successful Bolshevik *coup* of October 1917 marked the beginning rather than the end of the Russian Revolution. The Bolsheviks under Lenin faced immense problems in trying to consolidate their hold over what had been the tsarist empire. At the beginning of 1918 three particularly urgent questions confronted the new regime. First – how were the Bolsheviks, in view of their meagre military resources, to extend their control over the nation at large? Second – how could they achieve a speedy end to the war and effect a rapid withdrawal of the German army which was currently occupying the greater part of western Russia? Third – how quickly, if at all, would they be able to bring economic stability to a Russia devastated by four years of war and internal upheaval?

These problems were so demanding that they allowed Lenin's government little opportunity to preside over a peaceful political transition. Beset by internal and external enemies, the Bolsheviks were engaged in a desperate struggle for survival. It has also to be remembered that in developing their government of Russia, the Bolsheviks were working from hand to mouth. They had few preconceived plans. Before 1917 their time had been spent in preparing for revolution. Comparatively little attention had been given to the details of how affairs would be organised once this had been achieved. It had always been a Marxist belief that after the final triumph of the proletariat the state would 'wither away'. Trotsky had expressed this simple faith at the time of his appointment in 1917 as commissar for foreign affairs when he said that all that was required to be done was 'to issue a few decrees, then shut up shop and go home'. In the event, circumstances did not allow such a relaxed approach to government.

Two developments obliged Lenin's government to adopt dictatorial control after 1917. One was internal, the other external, but the Bolsheviks interpreted them as part of one grand design. The internal threat took the form of a Russian civil war, fought between 1918 and 1920, in which the Bolsheviks (the Reds) were confronted by a loose combination of anti-Bolshevik forces (the Whites). The external threat came in 1918–19 with a series of military interventions in Russia by a number of foreign powers, including Britain, France, the USA and Japan.

1 The Dissolution of the Constituent Assembly

Lenin was never a democrat in the simple sense of believing in the principle of 'one man, one vote'. He dismissed this as 'bourgeois democracy'. For him, true democracy was the rule of the Bolshevik Party, the voice of the revolutionary masses. This idea was based on the notion that the workers needed the enlightened leadership of the Bolsheviks to guide them towards the achievement of their revolutionary potential. It followed that the Bolshevik Party had both the duty to direct the workers and the right to obedience from them. This particular interpretation of democracy, often referred to as 'democratic centralism', also left Lenin free to disregard election results if they did not accord with his perception of the needs of the revolution or the party. Lenin had never had any great faith in mere numbers: his objective had not been to win mass support but to create a party capable of seizing power when the political circumstances permitted. This was why he had refused to join a broad-front opposition movement before 1917, and why, after the February Revolution, he had consistently opposed any form of co-operation with the Provisional Government. After the successful October *coup* in 1917 he was even more determined not to jeopardise the Bolsheviks' newly-won power by allowing elections to dictate the pace of revolutionary change. The results of the November 1917 election to the Constituent Assembly, therefore, presented him with an immediate problem. They revealed that the Bolsheviks had won barely a quarter of the seats.

Results of the election for the Constituent Assembly, November 1917

	Votes	Seats
SRs	17,490,000	370
Bolsheviks	9,844,000	175
National minority groups	8,257,000	99
Left SRs (pro-Bolshevik)	2,861,000	40
Kadets (Constitutional Democrats)	1,986,000	17
Mensheviks	1,248,000	16
Total	41,686,000	717

* Lenin had originally supported the idea of a Constituent Assembly, but he now calculated that it would be impossible for his party to govern effectively alongside an assembly that was overwhelmingly non-Bolshevik. His response was simple and unscrupulous. In January 1918, after only one day's session, the Constituent Assembly was dissolved at gun-point by the Red Guards. This act of violence has to be viewed in context. The Bolsheviks' hold on power was precarious. Indeed, the prospects of Bolshevik survival at all seemed slim. There was strong and widespread opposition to them inside the country, and Russia was still at war with Germany, with the allies all set to interfere should the new Russian government contemplate making a separate

peace. In such an atmosphere, the Bolsheviks were not prepared to entertain thoughts of power-sharing. Lenin justified the Bolshevik action in the following terms:

1 To hand over power to the Constituent Assembly would again be compromising with the malignant bourgeoisie. The Russian Soviets place the interests of the toiling masses far above the interests of treacherous compromise disguised in a new garb. A
5 musty spirit of antiquity breathed in the speeches of those superannuated politicians, Chernov [leader of the SRs] and Tseretelli [a leading Menshevik], who continued tediously to whine for the cessation of civil war. But as long as behind the slogan 'All power to the Constituent Assembly' is concealed the
10 slogan 'Down with the Soviets', civil war is inevitable. For nothing in the world will induce us to surrender the Soviet power. And when the Constituent Assembly again revealed its readiness to postpone all the painfully urgent problems and tasks that were placed before it by the soviets, we told the Constituent Assembly
15 that they must not be postponed for a single moment. And by the will of the Soviet power, the Constituent Assembly, which has refused to recognise the power of the people, is dissolved. The Soviet Revolutionary Republic will triumph no matter what the cost.

Commenting on Lenin's attitude at this stage, Trotsky observed that 'Lenin's theoretical considerations went hand in hand with the use of sharpshooters'. He recorded a remark Lenin had made to him in private: 'The dissolution of the Constituent Assembly by the Soviet Government means a complete and frank liquidation of the idea of democracy by the idea of dictatorship.'

In the historical debate over Lenin as a revolutionary, his sympathisers have often argued that the oppressive character of Soviet Communism in action was not the fault of Lenin but of Joseph Stalin, who corrupted the essentially democratic nature of the Revolution begun in 1917. The violent dissolution of the Constituent Assembly is one of a number of incidents that contradict this claim. It reveals Lenin as being ruthless in his determination to crush opposition to Bolshevik rule. Maxim Gorky, a Bolshevik intellectual, wrote at the time:

1 The best Russians have lived for almost 100 years with the idea of a Constituent Assembly as a political organ which could provide Russian democracy as a whole with the possibility of freely exercising its will. On the altar of this sacred idea rivers of blood
5 have been spilled – and now the 'people's commissars' have ordered the shooting of this democracy.

Many foreign communists were appalled by Lenin's behaviour. Rosa Luxemburg, a German socialist, commented bitterly:

1 To be sure, every democratic institution has its limitations. But the remedy which Lenin and Trotsky have found, the elimination of democracy itself, is worse than the disease it is supposed to cure; for it stops up the very living source from which alone can
5 come the correction of all the shortcomings of social institutions. That source is the active, untrammelled, energetic, political life of the broadest masses of the people.

2 The Treaty of Brest-Litovsk 1918

There was a marked difference of attitude between Lenin and Trotsky over the way in which the war with Germany should be ended. Lenin wanted an immediate peace; Trotsky wanted a delay. Lenin's thinking appears to have run along the following lines. Russia's military exhaustion made it impossible for her to fight on successfully. If Germany eventually won the war on both fronts she would retain the Russian territory that she now possessed. But if Germany lost the war against the Western Allies, Russia would regain her occupied lands. In the first eventuality, Russia would not be worse off; in the second she would actually gain, so what point was there in pretending she could continue the war?

There is also a strong likelihood that Lenin's readiness to make peace with Germany was not wholly ideological. Between 1914 and 1917 the German Foreign Office had given substantial and regular financial support to Lenin and the Bolsheviks in the hope that if they achieved their revolutionary aims they would pull Russia out of the war. This fact had been well-known. What was less obvious, and became fully established only after the examination by western analysts in 1945 of captured German foreign-policy documents of the First World War period, was that Germany continued to finance Lenin even after the October Revolution and the armistice of December 1917. It is highly likely, therefore, that to Lenin's perception of Russia's incapacity to fight on was added an understandable desire not to dry up this considerable source of Bolshevik revenue by unnecessarily offending his paymasters.

Trotsky also accepted that Bolshevik Russia had no realistic chance of continuing the military struggle against Germany. However, in the hope that within a short time the German armies would collapse on the western front and revolution would follow in Germany, he determined to make the peace talks a long, protracted affair. This approach, for which he coined the slogan 'no peace, no war', was intended to confuse and infuriate the German delegation and to buy more time for Bolshevik agitators to exploit the mutinous tendencies in the Austro-

German armies. In effect, Trotsky took a middle position between Lenin, who had wanted peace immediately, and those Bolsheviks and Left Revolutionaries who were pressing for the continuation of the war as a revolutionary crusade against imperialist Germany. At Brest-Litovsk, the Polish town where the Germans and Russians gathered to discuss peace terms, Trotsky chose deliberately to embarrass and annoy the German delegation. He showed his contempt for what he called 'bourgeois propriety' by consistently flouting the accepted rules of European diplomacy. Germany's chief negotiator, Field-Marshal Hindenburg, complained that 'Trotsky degraded the conference-table to the level of a tub-thumper's street corner'. He bemoaned the fact that 'Lenin and Trotsky behaved more like victors than vanquished, while trying to sow the seeds of political dissolution in the ranks of our army'.

* What Hindenburg and the Germans had not grasped was that Trotsky and Lenin did indeed see themselves as victors – potential if not actual. They were not perturbed by the thought of national defeat. Their spirits were buoyed up by the belief that time and history were on their side. They believed that a great international political victory was imminent. It is important to remember that Lenin and Trotsky, as international revolutionaries, had only a limited loyalty towards Russia as a nation. Their first concern was to spread the anticipated proletarian revolution elsewhere.

This readiness to subordinate Russian national interests explains why, to the dismay of most Russians and many Bolsheviks, the Soviet delegation at Brest-Litovsk was eventually willing to sign a devastating peace treaty as soon as it became clear that the exasperated Germans were preparing to renew hostilities. Even so, Trotsky's international-revolutionary outlook did not prevent him from scoring a sharp nationalist propaganda point. Before signing the treaty on 3 March 1918 Sokolnikov, the Soviet representative, declared, under instructions from Trotsky, that it was not a freely-negotiated settlement but a German *Diktat* imposed on a helpless Russia. Weight was given to this claim by the terms of the treaty, which could hardly have been more humiliating for Russia. A huge slice of territory, amounting to a third of European Russia, stretching from the Baltic to the Black Sea and including the Ukraine, Russia's major grain-source, was ceded to Germany or her allies. The land lost – about a million square kilometres – contained a population of 45 million. In addition, Russia was required to pay three billion roubles in war reparations. Aware that the signing of the treaty would be resented by many Bolsheviks, who were urging a revolutionary struggle against Germany, Lenin stressed that his policy was the only realistic one.

1 Our impulse tells us to rebel, to refuse to sign this robber peace.
  Our reason will in our calmer moments tell us the plain naked
  truth – that Russia can offer no physical resistance because she is

materially exhausted by three-years' war. It is true that there may
5 be people who are willing to fight and die in a great cause. But
they are romanticists, who would sacrifice themselves without
prospects of real advantage. Wars are won today, not by enthusiasm alone, but by technical skill, railways, abundance of
supplies. Has the Russian Revolution any of these in the face of
10 an enemy equipped with all the techniques of bourgeois 'civilisa-
tion'? The Russian Revolution must sign the peace to obtain a
breathing space to recuperate for the struggle. The central point
of the world struggle now is the rivalry between English and
German finance-capital. Let the Revolution utilise this struggle
15 for its own ends.

* Despite the power of his argument, Lenin still experienced great
difficulty in convincing his colleagues. The issue was argued bitterly in
the Central Committee. In the end, Lenin gained his way only by
brow-beating and threatening to resign, and then only by a majority of
one in a crucial Committee division. Among those who voted with him
for the acceptance of the treaty were Trotsky, Stalin and Zinoviev;
among those who opposed him were Bukharin, Kamenev and Dzerzhinsky. A profound issue lay at the base of Bolshevik disagreements.
To understand this, it has to be re-emphasised that Lenin and Trotsky
were primarily international revolutionaries. For them Russia was a
means to an end – worldwide proletarian revolution. They expected
workers' risings, based on the Russian model, to sweep across Europe.
Purely national conflicts would soon be superseded by the international
class struggle of the workers. Lenin and Trotsky regarded the crippling
terms of the Treaty of Brest-Litovsk as of small account when set
against the great sweep of imminent world revolution.

Not all Bolsheviks shared this vision. There remained those in the
party (referred to as 'Left Communists') who were convinced that their
first task was to consolidate the October Revolution by driving out the
German imperialists. It was only Lenin's insistence on the absolute
need for party loyalty in a time of crisis that finally persuaded such
Bolsheviks to subordinate their patriotic feelings to their political
ideology. Serious opposition to Lenin's leadership might well have
persisted had not the turn of military events in western Europe saved
the day. What eventually destroyed the argument of the Left Communists and the Left SRs, and proved the shrewdness of Lenin's original
reasoning, was the collapse of Germany's western front in August 1918,
followed by the almost total withdrawal of German forces from Russia.
Lenin's gamble that circumstances would soon make the Treaty of
Brest-Litovsk meaningless had paid off. It strengthened his hold over
the party and provided the opportunity to expel the Left SRs from the
government and to outlaw them politically.

3 The Civil War 1918–20

Since civil wars are not formally declared, it is seldom possible to give a precise date for their beginning. The consensus among historians with regard to the Russian Civil War is that it began in the summer of 1918. It was not just a matter of the Bolsheviks facing their political enemies in military struggle. From the outset the Civil War was a much more complex affair. The Bolsheviks presented it as a class war, but it was never simply this. The sheer size of Russia often meant that local or regional considerations predominated over larger ideological issues. Significantly, a number of Russia's national minorities, such as the Ukrainians and the Georgians, fought in the war with the aim of establishing their independence from Russia. These national forces became known as the Greens. The best-known of the Green leaders was Makhno, a one-time Bolshevik, who organised a guerilla resistance to the Reds in the Ukraine.

It was ironic that, although most of the leading Bolsheviks were non-Russian, their rule was seen by many as yet another attempt to re-assert Russian authority over the rest of the country – the very situation that had prevailed under the tsars. As in all civil wars, the disruption provided a cover for settling old scores and pursuing personal vendettas, and it was not uncommon for villages or families to be divided against each other. On occasion, the fighting was simply a struggle for food supplies. It has to be remembered that famine provided the backdrop to the Civil War. The dislocation of supplies that had occurred during the war against Germany had still to be rectified. Until this was done whole areas of Russia remained in a desperate economic plight.

The failure of the new regime to deal adequately with the country's most pressing needs was an important factor in creating the initial military opposition to the Bolsheviks in 1918. In addition to the problems of a fractured transport system, Lenin's government was faced with the loss of Russia's main wheat-supply area, the Ukraine, which was formally annexed by Germany under the terms of the Treaty of Brest-Litovsk. In the month in which the treaty was signed, the bread ration in Petrograd reached its lowest ever allocation of 50 grams per day. Hunger drove many workers out of the major industrial cities. By June 1918 the workforce in Petrograd had shrunk by 60 per cent and the overall population had declined from three to two millions. A visitor to the city at this time spoke of 'entering a metropolis of cold, of hunger, of hatred, of endurance'. The Bolshevik boast that October 1917 had established worker-control of Russian industry meant little now that the workers were deserting the factories in droves.

* These dire circumstances encouraged open challenges to the Bolsheviks from both left and right. SRs, who had been driven from the government following their refusal to accept the Brest-Litovsk settlement, attempted to stage a *coup* in the Moscow Soviet. (In 1918 for security reasons Moscow replaced Petrograd as the capital of Soviet Russia.) This failed, but their terrorist tactics were more successful. Lenin only narrowly survived two SR attempts on his life, in July and August, while two Bolshevik Party bosses were assassinated during the same period. In their desperation at being denied any say in government, the SRs, despite their deep ideological differences with the Whites, joined them in common cause against Lenin's Reds in the Civil War.

Armed resistance to the Bolsheviks had occurred sporadically in various parts of Russia since the October *coup*. What gave focus to this struggle was the behaviour in the summer of 1918 of one of the foreign armies still inside Russia. A contingent of 40,000 Czechoslovak troops, who had volunteered to fight on the Russian side in the First World War as a means of gaining independence from Austria-Hungary, found themselves isolated after the Treaty of Brest-Litovsk. They formed themselves into the Czech Legion and decided to make the long journey eastwards to Vladivostok. Their aim was eventually to rejoin the allies on the western front in the hope of winning international support for the formation of an independent Czechoslovak state. The presence of this well-equipped foreign army making its way arrogantly across Russia was not welcome to the Bolsheviks. Local soviets began to

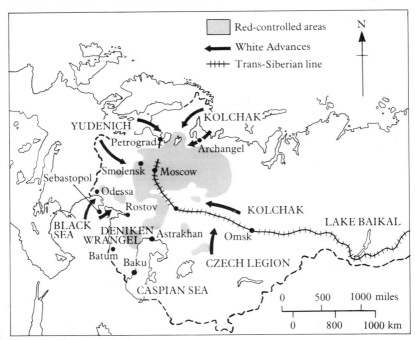

The Civil War 1918–20

challenge the Czech Legion and fierce fighting accompanied its progress along the trans-Siberian railway. All this encouraged the Whites and those groups who had been dispossessed by the dissolution of the Constituent Assembly, such as the SRs and the Kadets, to come out openly against Lenin's regime. The SRs organised a number of uprisings in central Russia and established an anti-Bolshevik Volga 'Republic' at Samara. A White 'Volunteer Army', led by General Denikin, had already been formed in the Caucasus region of southern Russia from tsarist loyalists and outlawed Kadets. In Siberia, the presence of the Czech Legion encouraged the formation of a White army under Admiral Kolchak, the self-proclaimed 'Supreme Ruler of Russia'. In Estonia, another ex-tsarist general, Yudenich, began to form a White army of resistance. White units appeared in many regions elsewhere. The speed with which they arose indicated just how limited Bolshevik control was outside the cities of western Russia.

  * The criss-cross of political, regional and national loyalties inside Russia, together with the added complication of the foreign interventions, made the Civil War a complex affair. It is best understood as a story of the Bolsheviks' resisting attacks on four main fronts, and then taking the initiative and driving back their attackers until they eventually withdrew or surrendered. Unlike the First World War, from which Soviet Russia had recently withdrawn, the Civil War was a war of movement, largely dictated by the layout of Russia's railway system. It was because the Bolsheviks were largely successful in their desperate fight to maintain control of the railway lines that they were able to keep themselves supplied, while denying the Whites the same benefit.

  The reasons for the final victory of the Reds in the Civil War are not difficult to determine. The various White armies fought as separate detachments. Apart from their obvious desire to overthrow the Bolsheviks, they were never bound together by a single aim. They were unwilling to sacrifice their individual interests in order to form a united anti-Bolshevik front. This allowed the Reds to pick off the White armies one by one. In the rare cases in which the Whites did consider co-operating, they were too widely scattered geographically to be able to bring sufficient pressure to bear on the enemy. The Reds, in contrast, remained in control of a concentrated central area of western Russia which they were able to defend by maintaining their inner communication and supply lines. The two major cities, Petrograd and Moscow, the administrative centres of Russia, remained in their hands throughout the war, as did the railway network. The Reds also possessed a key advantage in that the areas where they had their strongest hold were the industrial centres of Russia. This gave them access to munitions and war supplies denied to the Whites. The consequent dependence of the Whites on supplies from abroad appeared to prove the Red accusation that they were in league with the foreign interventionists. The Civil War had produced a paradoxical situation in which the Reds were able to stand as champions of the Russian nation as well as proletarian revolutionaries.

Although the Reds imposed a reign of terror (see pages 118–122), the Whites were unable to capitalise on this in propaganda terms. Their own record of ill-treatment of local populations was as notorious as that of the Reds. To the ordinary Russian there was little to choose between the warring sides in regard to their brutality. It was not, therefore, that the Reds were genuinely popular. Indeed, by the end of the Civil War whatever initial peasant sympathy they had gained had been lost by the severity of their grain-requisitioning methods. It was that the Whites failed to present themselves as a better alternative. All that they could offer was a return to the pre-revolutionary past. This was particularly damaging to them in relation to the land question. The Reds continually pointed out that all the lands which the peasants had seized in the Revolutions of 1917 would be forfeit if ever the Whites regained power. It was this fear more than any other that stopped the peasants from giving their support to the Whites.

* In the final assessment, the outstanding factor explaining the success of the Reds in the Civil War was their driving sense of purpose. Waging war is not just a matter of resources and fire-power. Morale and dedication play an equally vital role. Trotsky may have been extreme in his methods, but he created an army which proved capable of fighting with an unshakable belief in its own eventual victory. Set against this, the Whites were never more than an unco-ordinated collection of separate forces, whose morale was never high. They were an uncertain grouping of dispossessed socialists, liberals, and moderates, whose political differences often led them into bitter disputes among themselves. Throughout the Civil War, the White cause was deeply divided by the conflicting interests of those who were fighting for local separatism and those who wanted a return to strong central government. Since they were without a common cause, other than their hatred of Bolshevism, the Whites lacked effective leadership. This was a problem they were unable to resolve. No White leader emerged of the stature of Trotsky or Lenin around whom an effective anti-Bolshevik army could unite.

4 The Foreign Interventions

When tsardom collapsed in Russia in 1917 the immediate response of the western allies was shaped less by political considerations than by military ones. Would the new regime keep Russia in the war? That was the vital question that preoccupied Britain and France. If Russia made a separate peace, Germany would be free to divert huge military resources from the eastern to the western front. To prevent this, the Allies offered large amounts of capital and military supplies to Russia, in return for a firm commitment from the Provisional Government to continue the war against Germany. Such a commitment was duly given by the new regime (see page 85).

Before 1914 little serious attention had been paid abroad to Bolshevism. What gave it greater international prominence was the onset of world war in 1914, a war which Lenin condemned as a capitalist struggle in which the workers would be used as cannon fodder. His unwavering determination to withdraw Russia from the war naturally excited German interest. The German government, through its secret service, consistently provided the Bolsheviks with financial aid in the hope of bringing about revolution and military collapse in Russia. The Bolshevik *coup* had precisely the effect hoped for by Germany and feared by the Allies. Within a few weeks an armistice had been agreed between Germany and the Bolshevik government, and fighting on the eastern front ceased in December 1917. The initial response of France and Britain was cautious. In the faint hope that the new regime might be persuaded to continue the fight against Germany, the same support was offered to the Bolshevik government as had been extended to its predecessors.

Lloyd George, the British prime minister, declared that he was neither for nor against Bolshevism, but simply anti-German, and therefore willing to side with any group in Russia, regardless of its politics, if it would commit itself to the war against Germany. However, in the circumstances prevailing in Russia, with Lenin refusing to consider a renewal of the fight against Germany, it so happened that any help given by Britain to anti-German Russians went necessarily to anti-Bolshevik forces. It appeared to the Bolsheviks that Britain and her allies were intent on destroying them. This was matched by the allies' view that in making a separate peace with Germany the Bolsheviks had acted as arch-traitors to the allied cause. The result was a fierce determination among the allies to prevent their vital war-supplies, previously loaned to Russia and still stock-piled there, from falling into German hands. British and French thoughts turned towards armed intervention.

* In March 1918, following the news of the signing of the Treaty of Brest-Litovsk, British, French and United States' detachments occupied the ports of Murmansk in the Arctic and Archangel in the White Sea.

This was the prelude to a two-year period during which armed contingents from a large number of countries occupied important areas of European, central and far-eastern Russia. No single aim united the interventionists. The declared motive of Britain, France, Germany, Italy, Japan and the USA was the legitimate protection of their individual interests. The objective of Czechoslovakia, Finland, Lithuania, Poland and Romania, all of whom directly bordered Russia, was to assert a claim, going back to tsarist times, to territorial independence from Russia. In 1918 British land forces entered Transcaucasia in southern Russia and also occupied part of Central Asia, while British warships sailed into Russian Baltic waters and into the Black Sea, where they were joined by French naval vessels. The French also established a major land base around the Black Sea port of Odessa. In April 1918, Japanese troops occupied Russia's chief far-eastern port of Vladivostok. Four months later, they were joined by units from France, Britain, the USA and Italy. In 1919 Japanese and United States troops occupied parts of Siberia.

These were not co-operative ventures. The separate forces were frequently as suspicious of each other as they were of the Bolsheviks. However, to the Bolsheviks, the claim of the major western powers to be concerned solely with the lawful recovery of their munitions was simply a pretext for an imperialist invasion of Russia aimed at overthrowing the Revolution. From that point on, the Bolsheviks made no distinction between the aims of their internal enemies, the Whites, and those of the foreign interventionists. With the close of the war on the western front in November 1918 there was a vociferous demand from fervent anti-Bolsheviks such as Churchill, the British cabinet minister, and Marshal Foch, the French military leader, that the wartime allies should unite in a major offensive against the Bolsheviks. They added weight to their appeals by referring to the spread of revolution to Germany, where in 1918–19 a short-lived Communist republic was established in Bavaria and a 'Spartacist' (Communist) rising occurred in Berlin, and also to Hungary, where early in 1919 Bela Kun led a successful Marxist *coup*. They could also point to Bolshevik terror tactics, highlighted by the murder of the ex-tsar and his family in July 1918 and to the direct threat to all nations posed by the creation in Moscow in 1919 of the Communist International (Comintern), the Bolshevik organisation formally dedicated to the fomenting of revolution in all other lands.

   * There was also a specifically financial aspect to anti-Bolshevism in western Europe. One of the first acts of the Bolshevik regime was to declare that the new government had no intention of honouring the foreign debts entered into by its predecessors. In addition, it nationalised a large number of foreign companies and froze all foreign assets in Russia. Those foreigners who had bought shares in imperial Russian enterprises or who had set up companies in Russia found their investments wiped out. The understandably bitter reaction to what was regarded as international theft was particularly strong in France where many small and middle-scale financiers had invested in pre-1914 Russia. It was the French who now took the lead in proposing an international campaign against the Bolsheviks. What prevented the proposal from being fully acted upon was the reluctance of Woodrow Wilson, the American president, to commit United States forces to such a scheme. American troops did intervene in Russia, but their presence was principally intended to deter the other foreign powers

from going too far. It was part of Woodrow Wilson's general policy, which he followed in the peace talks at Versailles in 1919, of trying to achieve moderation and compromise in the post-war settlement of Europe.

Despite the preaching of an anti-Bolshevik crusade by influential voices in western Europe, no concerted attempt was made to unseat the Bolshevik regime. This was shown by the relative ease with which the interventions were resisted. The truth was that the interventionist nations were war-weary after four long years of struggle against Germany. They had no stomach for a prolonged campaign. There were serious threats of mutiny in some British and French regiments ordered to embark for Russia. Trade unionists, who at this stage were sympathetic towards the new 'workers' state', were reluctant to load or transport military supplies bound for Russia. Even when the interventionist forces did arrive in Russia, there was seldom effective liaison between the various national contingents. Moreover, such efforts as they made to co-operate with the White armies already engaged in the Civil War were half-hearted and ineffectual. The one major exception to this was in the Baltic states where the national forces, backed by British warships and troops, crushed a Bolshevik invasion and obliged Lenin's government to recognise the independence of Estonia, Latvia and Lithuania, a freedom which they maintained until taken over by Stalin in 1940.

Such interventionist success was not repeated elsewhere. After a token display of aggression the foreign troops began everywhere to withdraw. By the end of 1919, all French and American troops had been recalled, and by the end of 1920, all other western contingents had left. It was only the Japanese who remained in Russia for the duration of the Civil War, finally leaving in 1922. In no real sense were these withdrawals a military victory for the Bolsheviks, but that was exactly how they were portrayed in Soviet propaganda. Lenin's government grasped the opportunity to present itself as the saviour of the nation from foreign conquest. This went a considerable way to recover the esteem it had lost over the 1918 capitulation to Germany. It helped to put resolve into the party members who had wavered and it lent credibility to the Bolshevik depiction of the Whites as agents of the foreign powers, intent on restoring reactionary tsardom.

5 The Effects of the Civil War

a) On Soviet Foreign Policy

The victory of the Bolsheviks in the Civil War encouraged them to undertake what proved to be a humiliatingly unsuccessful attempt to expand their authority beyond Soviet Russia's western border. In 1920 the Red Army marched into neighbouring Poland in the expectation that the Polish workers would rise in rebellion against their own government. However, the Poles confounded the hopes of the Reds by interpreting the invasion as traditional Russian aggression. They unceremoniously drove the Red Army out. Soviet morale was seriously damaged, forcing Lenin and the Bolsheviks to rethink their role as organisers of international revolution.

Lenin adopted an essentially realistic approach. He judged that the Polish reverse, the foreign interventions in Russia, and the failure of the attempted Communist revolutions in Germany and Hungary all showed that the time was not ripe for world revolution. The capitalist nations were still too strong. In view of this hard reality, the Bolsheviks would not attempt the impossible. Without abandoning their long-term revolutionary objectives, they would adjust their foreign policy to meet the new situation. Notwithstanding the existence of the Comintern, which continued to call for world revolution, Soviet Russia greatly softened its attitude towards other countries. This re-orientation was defined by Lenin in 1921. 'Our foreign policy while we are alone and while the capitalist world is strong consists in our exploiting contradictions.' Lenin meant by this that for as long as the international situation made socialist revolution unattainable, Soviet Russia would protect herself by playing on the differences that divided the capitalist nations from each other. He calculated that their commercial and military self-interests would keep them apart. It should, therefore, be Soviet policy to do nothing that would frighten such countries as France, Britain and Germany into suspending their rivalry in favour of an anti-Bolshevik alliance.

Lenin's concerns were very much in the tradition of Russian foreign policy. Western encroachment into Russia had been a constant fear of the tsars. That long-standing Russian worry had been increased by the intensely hostile response of European governments to the October Revolution and by their support of the Whites during the Civil War. Lenin's reading of the international situation led him to conclude that discretion was the better part of valour. Under him Soviet foreign policy was activated not by thoughts of expansion but by the desire to avoid conflict.

b) On Internal Affairs

The Civil War was one of the great formative influences on the Bolshevik Party. Their attempts to come to terms with the reality of power and learn how to govern took place in a period of disruption and chaos in which the very survival of Bolshevism long remained in doubt. The development of the party and the government have to be set against such a background. The Revolution had been born in war, and the government had been formed in war. During the course of the Civil War half a million members of the party fought in the Red Army.

Calculations show that of all the members of the Communist Party in 1927, a third had joined in the years 1917–20. This had created a tradition of military obedience and loyalty.

A number of modern analysts have emphasised the central place that the Civil War had in shaping the character of Communist rule in Soviet Russia. Robert Tucker stresses that it was the military aspect of early Bolshevik government that left it with a 'readiness to resort to coercion, rule by administrative fiat, centralised administration [and] summary justice'. This is not to deny that Lenin's brand of applied Marxism was essentially totalitarian, but it is to suggest that no regime placed in the Bolshevik predicament between 1917 and 1921 could have survived without resort to authoritarian measures. By way of illustration, it could be argued that the major reason for the failure of the Provisional Government in 1917 had been its reluctance to take the firm steps necessary for its survival.

The move towards centralism in government became increasingly marked as the Civil War dragged on. Equally significant was the same centralising process within the government itself. The emergencies of war required immediate day-to-day decisions to be made. This led to effective power moving away from the Central Committee of the Communist (Bolshevik) Party, which was too cumbersome, into the hands of the two major sub-committees, the Politburo and the Orgburo, which, being smaller and more tightly knit, could act with the necessary speed. In practice the authority of Sovnarkom, the official government of Soviet Russia, became indistinguishable from the rule of these party committees.

The centralising of authority was also evident in the official renaming in 1922 of the Soviet state as the the USSR (Union of Soviet Socialist Republics). This new constitution replaced the looser RSFSR (Russian Socialist Federal Soviet Republic), which had been adopted in 1918. E. H. Carr comments: 'the USSR was little more than the RSFSR writ large, and represented an extension of the central authority of Moscow'.

6 The Terror

The repression that characterised the imposition of Bolshevik control over Russia became known as the Terror. Some writers argue that it was the scale of the problems confronting the Bolsheviks after the October Revolution that explains, and indeed justifies, the extreme measures which Lenin's government adopted. Others assert that repression is a necessary and unavoidable part of any political creed such as Marxism-Leninism, which regards itself as uniquely superior to all other ideologies. Lenin had always accepted the necessity of terror as an instrument of political control. Before 1917 he had often made it clear that a Marxist revolution could not survive if it were not prepared to crush its enemies:

1 Coercion is necessary for the transition from capitalism to socialism. The form of coercion is determined by the degree of
development of the given revolutionary class, and also by special
circumstances, such as, for example, the heritage of a long and
5 reactionary war and the forms of resistance put up by the
bourgeoisie. Hence there is absolutely no contradiction between
Soviet democracy and the exercise of dictatorial powers.

The chief instruments by which the Bolsheviks exercised their policy of
terror were the *Cheka* and the Red Army.

a) The *Cheka*

In practice, the *Cheka* was essentially a better organised and more
efficient form of the *Okhrana*, the former tsarist secret police, at whose
hands nearly every Bolshevik activist had previously suffered. An idea
of its purpose can be judged from its full title, 'the All-Russian
Extraordinary Commission for Fighting Counter-Revolution, Sabotage
and Speculation'. It was created in December 1917 and was headed by
Felix Dzerzhinsky, a Polish intellectual of aristocratic birth who sought
to atone for his privileged origins by absolute dedication to the
Bolshevik cause. Lenin found him the ideal choice to lead the fight
against the enemies of the Revolution because Dzerzhinsky never
allowed finer feelings or a sense of compassion to deter him from the
task of destroying the real or potential opponents of the Bolshevik
regime. His remorseless attitude was shown in the various directives
that issued from the *Cheka* headquarters in Moscow.

1 Our Revolution is in danger. Do not concern yourselves with the
forms of revolutionary justice. We have no need for justice now.
Now we have need of a battle to the death! I propose, I demand
the use of the revolutionary sword which will put an end to all
5 counter-revolutionaries.

Exploiting each attempt on the part of individuals or groups to
challenge Bolshevik rule, the *Cheka*, always with Lenin's full backing,
set about spreading a network of terror across the greater part of
Russia. In July 1918 a group of SRs assassinated the German ambassador as a protest against the Treaty of Brest-Litovsk. A month later an
attempt was made on Lenin's life by an SR sympathiser, followed by
the murder of the Petrograd chairman of the *Cheka*. These incidents
were made the pretext for a Bolshevik reign of terror. It was in this
atmosphere that a local *Cheka* detachment took it upon itself in July
1918 to execute the ex-tsar, Nicholas, and his family in Ekaterinburg.
The summary shooting of the Romanovs without benefit of trial was
typical of the manner in which the *Cheka* went about its business

throughout Russia. In accordance with Dzerzhinsky's instructions, all pretence of legality was abandoned; the basic rules relating to evidence and proof of guilt ceased to exist. Persecution was directed not simply against individuals, but against whole classes. This was class war of the most direct kind.

1 Do not demand incriminating evidence to prove that the prisoner has opposed the Soviet government by force or words. Your first duty is to ask him to which class he belongs, what are his origins, his education, his occupation. These questions should decide the
5 fate of the prisoner.

* The savagery of the *Cheka*'s methods led to protests from within the Bolshevik Party (renamed the Communist Party in 1919), concerning the abandonment of 'socialist legality'. Had circumstances allowed, there might well have been attempts from within the party to restrict the powers of the *Cheka*, but so hazardous was the situation between 1918 and 1921 that the majority of members believed that severe repression was justified. The foreign interventions and the Civil War, fought out against the background of famine and imminent economic collapse, threatened to destroy the very existence of the Communist Party and the government. This had the effect of stifling serious criticism of the methods used to achieve survival. Dzerzhinsky was convinced that the proletarian revolution could not be saved except by 'exterminating the enemies of the working class'. This was an exact echo of Lenin's words: 'This is an arch-war situation. We must work up energy and mass-like terror against counter-revolutionaries.'

b) The Red Army

The creation of the Red Army was the work of Trotsky, who, after the signing of the Treaty of Brest-Litovsk, became commissar for war. Lenin showed his complete trust in Trotsky by giving him a wholly free hand in military matters. From his heavily-armed special train, which served as his military headquarters and steamed over vast distances, Trotsky supervised the formation and administration of a new fighting force in Russia. He had inherited 'The Workers' and Peasants' Red Army', formed early in 1918. Within two years he had turned an unpromising collection of tired Red Guard veterans and raw recruits into a formidable army of three million men. Ignoring the objections of many fellow Bolsheviks, he enlisted large numbers of ex-tsarist officers to train the rank and file into efficient soldiers. As a precaution, Trotsky attached political commissars to the army. These became an integral part of the Red Army structure. The commissars were dedicated Party workers whose function was to accompany the officers permanently and report on their reliability and political correctness. No military order carried final authority unless it was countersigned by a political commissar.

Trotsky tolerated no opposition within the Red Army from officers or men. The death sentence was imposed for desertion or disloyalty. In accordance with revolutionary principles, an attempt had been made initially to dispense with the traditional forms of army discipline. Graded ranks, special uniforms, saluting and deferential titles were jettisoned as belonging to the reactionary past. However, within a short time the demands of war rendered such experiments too dangerous. Trotsky judged that tighter not looser discipline was needed. Although the term 'officer' was replaced by 'commander', in all other key respects the Red Army returned to the customary forms of rank and address, with the word 'Comrade' usually prefixing the standard terms, as in 'Comrade Captain'. The practice of electing officers, which had come into favour in the democratic atmosphere of the February Revolution, was abandoned, as were soldiers' committees.

Trotsky responded to the Civil War's increasing demand for more manpower by enforcing conscription in those areas under Bolshevik control. (The Whites attempted the same in their areas.) Using the slogan 'Everything for the Front', Trotsky justified the severity of the Red Army's methods by referring to the dangers that Russia faced on all sides. Those individuals whose social or political background made them suspect as fighting-men were conscripted, nonetheless, and formed into labour battalions for back-breaking service behind the lines. The peasants conscripted into the Red Army were for the most part reluctant warriors, and were not regarded as reliable in a crisis. Desertions were commonplace, in spite of the heavy penalties. The Bolsheviks judged that the only dependable units were those drawn predominantly from among the workers. Such units became in practice the elite corps or shock troops of the Red Army. Heroic stories of the workers as defenders of the Revolution rapidly spread. Moreover, not everything was achieved by coercion; there were idealists among the troops, who believed sincerely in the mission of Bolshevism to create a new proletarian world. Theirs was a vital contribution to the relatively high morale of the Reds. Although by the standards of the European armies of the time the Red Army did not compare well in regard to equipment and expertise, within Russia it soon came to outstrip its White opponents in terms of fighting efficiency and sense of purpose.

Throughout the Civil War, Reds and Whites continually accused each other of committing atrocities. Both were right. Both sides did undoubtedly use terror as a means of crushing opposition in the areas they seized. The actual fighting seems not to have been unduly bloody; it was in the aftermath, when the civilian population was cowed into submission, that the savagery usually occurred. The Reds gained recruits by offering defeated enemy troops and uncommitted civilians the choice of enlisting or being executed.

Trotsky's strategic objectives were relatively simple and direct: to defend the Red Army's internal lines of communication, to deny the Whites the opportunity to concentrate large forces in any one location, and to prevent them from maintaining regular supplies. The key to this was control of Russia's railways. Trotsky viewed the role of the railways as equivalent to that of the cavalry in former times. They were the means of transporting troops swiftly and in large numbers to the critical areas of defence or attack. It was no accident that the decisive confrontations between Reds and Whites took place near rail heads and depots. Trotsky's broad strategy proved successful. Once the Reds had established an impregnable defence of their inner lines, they were able to exhaust the enemy as an attacking force and then drive them back on the major fronts until they disengaged and scattered or sued for peace.

Notwithstanding Trotsky's overwhelming success as a military organiser and strategist, his authority did not go unchallenged. It was not unknown for him to meet opposition from local Red commanders and commissars over tactics. His most notable dispute was with Stalin, who acted as political commissar in the Caucasus. Their legendary personal hostility dates from the Civil War days. Nonetheless, whatever the disputes, there was no serious doubting that as the organising genius behind the Red Army, Trotsky's contribution to the eventual triumph of the Bolsheviks in the war was unmatchable.

7 The Kronstadt Rising 1921

The victory of the Red Army in the Civil War did not mark the end of open opposition to the Bolsheviks. 'War communism' (see page 131) involved the systematic use of terror by the *Cheka*, the spying on factory workers by political commissars, and the enforced requisitioning of peasant grain stocks at a time of widespread famine. As a short-term measure it produced the results Lenin wanted, but its severity was bound to increase Bolshevik unpopularity. Throughout 1920 there were outbreaks of resistance, the most serious occurring in the central Russian province of Tambov. As long as unrest was confined to the peasants and to the Bolsheviks' political enemies it was felt to be a containable problem. What became deeply worrying to Lenin and his governmental colleagues in 1921 was the development of opposition to war communism within the party itself. Two prominent Bolsheviks, Shlyapnikov, the labour commissar, and Alexandra Kollontai, the outstanding female in the party, led a 'Workers Opposition' movement against the excesses of war communism. Kollontai stated her position in a published pamphlet in which she declared that the party leaders were losing touch with the proletariat:

1 The workers ask – who are we? Are we really the prop of the class dictatorship, or just an obedient flock that serves as a support for

those, who having severed all ties with the masses, carry out their
own policy and build up industry without any regard to our
5 opinions and creative abilities under the reliable cover of the party
label.

Picking up the cue given by the 'Workers' Opposition', groups of
workers in Petrograd went on strike, justifying their actions in an
angrily worded declaration:

1 A complete change is necessary in the policies of the Government.
First of all, the workers and peasants need freedom. They don't
want to live by the decrees of the Bolsheviks; they want to control
their own destinies. Comrades, preserve revolutionary order!
5 Determinedly and in an organised manner demand: liberation of
all the arrested Socialists and non-partisan working-men; abolition of martial law; freedom of speech, press and assembly for all
who labour.

By February 1921 Petrograd workers in their thousands had crossed
to the naval base on Kronstadt. There they linked up with the sailors
and dockyard workers to demonstrate for greater freedom. They
demanded that in a workers' state, which the Bolshevik government
claimed Soviet Russia to be, the workers should be better, not worse off
than in tsarist times. The political commissars, sent from Petrograd by
Lenin in an attempt to pacify the strikers, were greeted with derision.
Petrechenko, a spokesman for the demonstrators, rounded on the
commissars at a public meeting:

1 You are comfortable; you are warm; you commissars live in the
palaces . . . Comrades, look around you and you will see that we
have fallen into a terrible mire. We were pulled into this mire by a
group of Communist bureaucrats, who, under the mask of
5 Communism, have feathered their nests in our republic. I myself
was a Communist, and I call on you, Comrades, drive out these
false Communists who set worker against peasant and peasant
against worker. Enough shooting of our brothers!

Early in March, the sailors and workers of Kronstadt elected Petrechenko as chairman of a 15-man Revolutionary Committee, responsible for representing their grievances to the government. This committee produced a manifesto which included the following demands:

1. New elections to the soviets, to be held by secret ballot.
2. Freedom of speech and of the press.
3. Freedom of assembly.
4. Rights for trade unions and release of imprisoned trade
unionists.

5. Ending of the right of Communists to be the only permitted socialist political party.
6. The release of left-wing political prisoners.
7. Ending of special food rations for Communist Party members.
8. Freedom for individuals to bring food from the country into the towns without confiscation.
9. Withdrawal of political commissars from the factories.
10. Ending of the Communist Party monopoly of the press.

* In responding to this manifesto, the chief concern of the Bolsheviks was not the demands themselves but their source. The workers and sailors of Kronstadt had been the great supporters of the Bolsheviks in 1917. Trotsky had referred to them as 'the heroes of the Revolution'. It was these same heroes who were now insisting that the Bolshevik government return to the promises that had inspired the Revolution. For all the efforts of the Bolshevik press to pretend that the Kronstadt protesters were White agents, the reality was that they were genuine socialists who had previously been wholly loyal to Lenin's government, but who had become appalled by the regime's betrayal of the workers' cause. Frightened by the growing number of strikers and angered by their increasing demands, Trotsky ordered the Red Army under General Tukhachevsky to cross the winter ice linking Kronstadt to Petrograd and to crush those whom he described as 'the tools of former tsarist generals' and 'agents of the interventionists'. An ultimatum was issued to the demonstrators. When this was rejected, Tukhachevsky gave the signal for his force, made up of Red Army units and *Cheka* detachments, to attack. After an artillery bombardment, 60,000 Red troops stormed the Kronstadt base. The sailors and workers resisted fiercely. Fighting of the most savage kind occurred before they were finally overcome. Tukhachevsky reported back to Trotsky:

1 The sailors fought like wild beasts. I cannot understand where they found the might for such rage. Each house where they were located had to be taken by storm. An entire company fought for an hour to capture one house and when the house was captured it
5 was found to contain two or three soldiers at a machine-gun. They seemed half-dead, but they snatched their revolvers and gasped, 'We didn't shoot enough at you bastards.'

Immediately after the rising had been crushed, the ring leaders who had survived were condemned as White reactionaries and shot. In the succeeding months the *Cheka* hunted down and executed those rebels who had tried to escape from Kronstadt. Lenin justified such severity on the grounds that the rising had been the work of the bourgeois enemies of the October Revolution: 'Both the Mensheviks and the

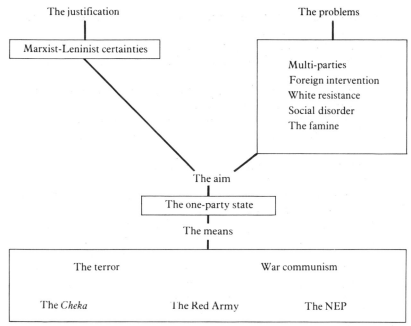

The justification

The problems

Marxist-Leninist certainties

Multi-parties
Foreign intervention
White resistance
Social disorder
The famine

The aim

The one-party state

The means

The terror   War communism

The *Cheka*   The Red Army   The NEP

Summary – The Bolshevik Consolidation of Power 1918–21

Socialist Revolutionaries declared the Kronstadt movement to be their own.' However, as well as being a propagandist, Lenin was also a realist. He took the lesson of Kronstadt to heart. He decided it was time to lessen the rigours of war communism in order to avoid another open challenge to his party and government. At the Tenth Conference of the Communist Party, which opened in March 1921, Lenin declared that the Kronstadt rising had 'lit up reality like a flash of lightning'. This was the prelude to his introduction of the New Economic Policy, a move intended to tackle the famine and in so doing to lessen the opposition to Bolshevism. However, this was to be a purely economic adjustment. Politically, Lenin made no concessions: the screw of Bolshevik control was turned even tighter.

Making notes on 'The Bolshevik Consolidation of Power 1918–21'

Your notes should cover the three years in question in chronological order and you should aim to provide yourself with a sound understanding of the military, political and economic problems confronting the Bolsheviks from 1917 onwards and the ways in which they attempted to deal with them. The economic aspects are treated in chapter 8 and you might be best advised to make your notes on the two chapters at the same time.

The following headings and questions indicate a possible method of assembling your material on the issues dealt with in this chapter.

Introduction: what were the most important problems confronting the Bolsheviks in the period 1918 to 1921?

1.   The Dissolution of the Constituent Assembly
1.1.   The reasons for, and consequences of, the dissolution
2.   The Treaty of Brest-Litovsk
2.1.   Trotsky's role as negotiator
2.2.   Why were Lenin and the Bolsheviks prepared to accept the treaty?
3.   The Civil War
3.1.   The variety of motives underlying the Civil War
3.2.   The role of the Czech Legion
3.3.   Why were the Reds victorious over the Whites?
4.   The Foreign Interventions
4.1.   The hostility of western governments towards Bolshevik Russia
4.2.   What form did foreign intervention take?
4.3.   Why did the interventions not succeed?
5.   The Effects of the Civil War
5.1.   How did the Civil War modify Bolshevik foreign policy?
5.2.   The effect of the Civil War in shaping Bolshevik domestic policy
6.   The Terror
6.1.   The character and function of the *Cheka*
6.2.   Trotsky's role as organiser of the Red Army
6.3.   The Red Army's success in crushing opposition
7.   The Kronstadt Rising
7.1.   The political significance of the Rising
7.2.   The manner of its suppression

Source-based on questions on 'The Bolshevik Consolidation of Power 1918–21'

1 The Dissolution of the Constituent Assembly
Study the election results on page 105, Lenin's statements on page 106, and the comments of Maxim Gorky and Rosa Luxemburg on page 107. Answer the following questions:
a) Account for the failure of the Bolsheviks to do as well as the SRs in the elections to the Constituent Assembly, as recorded in the table on page 105. (5 marks)
b) According to the argument put forward in the extracts on page 106,

what was Lenin's justification for the dissolution of the Constituent Assembly? (6 marks)
c) In what respects do the interpretations of democracy expressed by Gorky and Luxemburg differ from those put forward by Lenin in his justification for the dissolution of the Constituent Assembly? (8 marks)

2 The Terror

Read the extracts from Lenin's writings on page 119, and from Dzerzhinsky's directives on pages 120 and 121. Answer the following questions:
a) Examine the meaning of the following reference: 'The form of coercion is determined by the degree of development of the given revolutionary class' (page 119, line 2). (3 marks)
b) Using your own knowledge, examine the ways in which the *Cheka* fulfilled Dzerzhinsky's instruction to launch a policy of 'exterminating the enemies of the working class' (page 120, line 23). (7 marks)
c) In what respects do Lenin's ideas and Dzerzhinsky's directives, as recorded in these sources, represent an ideology of terror? (8 marks)

3 The Kronstadt Rising

Study the extracts from Kollontai's pamphlet on page 122, from the workers' declaration, from Petrochenko's speech, and from the ten demands on page 123. Answer the following questions:
a) In what ways do Kollontai's pamphlet and the workers' declaration suggest that Lenin's government had failed to keep its revolutionary promises? (5 marks)
b) Explain the meanings of the following terms as used by Petrechenko in his speech: 'commissars' (line 1); 'Communist bureaucrats' (line 4). (4 marks)
c) How far do the grievances listed in the ten-point manifesto correspond with the complaints voiced in the other three sources? (6 marks)
d) Using your own knowledge and the evidence in all the sources, comment on the view that the Kronstadt Rising was 'a struggle of real Communism against false Communism'. (9 marks)

CHAPTER 8

The Bolsheviks and the Economy 1918–24

In the period between the October Revolution of 1917 and the death of Lenin in 1924 there were three distinct and consecutive periods of Bolshevik economic policy: state capitalism, which operated from November 1917 to June 1918; war communism, which was imposed between 1918 and 1921; and the New Economic Policy, which was introduced in 1921 and was still operative in 1924.

These different stages did not mark an ordered, planned progression. Throughout the period, the Bolsheviks struggled to retain control of an economic situation with which their training as revolutionaries had not prepared them to deal. As with the technique of government and administration, they had to learn the skills of economic management as they went along. Few neutral historians now accept the traditional pro-Soviet view that under Lenin's inspired guidance the revolutionary government after 1917 embarked on a measured policy by which the Russian economy was successfully transformed into a planned socialist system in accordance with Marxist principles. Commentators now tend to interpret Lenin's policy as essentially one of adjustment to circumstances which, contrary to his original expection, soon proved to be beyond the resources of the Bolsheviks to command.

1 State Capitalism 1917–18

The Bolsheviks inherited huge economic problems in 1917. In theory, the October Revolution had marked the victory of proletarian socialism over bourgeois capitalism, but theory was of little immediate assistance in the circumstances of late 1917. Before the October Revolution, Lenin had written powerfully against landlords and grasping capitalists, but he had produced little in the way of genuine economic planning. It is understandable, therefore, that his policy after taking power in 1917 was a pragmatic one. He argued that the change from a bourgeois to a proletarian economy could not be achieved overnight. It necessitated a period during which the Bolshevik government would continue to use the existing economic structures until such time as the transition had been completed and a fully-fledged socialist system could be adopted. This transitional stage was referred to as 'state capitalism'. Lenin justified it to his colleagues in the following terms:

1 Without the guidance of specialists, no transition to socialism is possible, because, as compared with capitalism, socialism requires a deliberate and forward mass movement towards higher

productivity of labour. But the majority of specialists are
5 bourgeois. For the present we shall have to adopt the old
bourgeois method and agree to pay higher salaries for the
'services' of the biggest bourgeois specialists. All who are familiar
with the situation see the necessity of such a measure, though not
all understand its significance for the proletarian state. Clearly it
10 is a compromise measure.

Lenin was aware that there were many Bolsheviks who wanted the
immediate introduction of a more sweeping revolutionary policy, but
he pointed out that the new regime simply did not possess the power to
impose it. Its authority did not run much beyond Petrograd and
Moscow. Until the Bolsheviks were able to establish a much wider
political and military control, their economic policy would have to take
account of the prevailing circumstances. The war against Germany and
Austria had brought Russia to the point of economic collapse. The
shortage of raw materials and the decline in the amount of capital
available for investment had reduced industrial production to two-
thirds of its 1914 level. Inflation had reached uncontrollable heights.
The transport system had been crippled, and grain supplies were over
13 million tons short of the figure required to meet the nation's basic
needs. Within a few months of the October Revolution, the food
crisis had been further deepened by the ceding of the Ukraine to
Germany. The loss to Russia of her richest grain-producing region was
a disaster.

It was the food-supply problem that dominated Lenin's economic
thinking after the Bolsheviks took power. Indeed, all his economic
policies from 1917 until his death can be seen as a response to the basic
question: how could Russia find enough supplies to feed herself? Lenin
was a realist on the peasant question. Although he considered that the
future lay with the industrial workers, he never lost sight of the fact that
the peasantry, who made up the mass of the population, were the food
producers. Since no advance of any kind could be sustained unless
Russia could feed herself, logic demanded that in the Bolshevik
treatment of the peasants the primary consideration must be how best
they could be induced or forced into becoming suppliers of adequate
quantities of food.

Immediately after coming to power, the new government introduced
two measures which are usually regarded as having initiated Bolshevik
economic policy. These were the 'Decree on Land' and the 'Decree on
Workers' Control', both issued in November 1917. However, these
were not so much new departures as formal recognitions of what had
already occurred. The key article of the land decree stated:

1 Private ownership of land shall be abolished for ever; land shall
   not be sold, purchased, leased, mortgaged, or otherwise alien-

ated. All land, whether state, crown, monastery, church, factory,
entailed, private, public, peasant, etc, shall be confiscated with-
5 out compensation and become the property of the whole people,
and pass into the use of all those who cultivate it.

In effect, the decree officially sanctioned what had been happening in
the countryside since the February Revolution: in many areas the
peasants had overthrown their landlords and occupied their property.
Lenin had earlier accepted this as a *fait accompli*. Since the Bolsheviks
had no land policy of their own, he had simply taken over that of the
SRs, turning 'Land to the Peasants' into a Bolshevik slogan (see page
90). The Decree on Workers' Control was also largely concerned with
authorising what had already occurred. During 1917 a large number of
factories had been taken over by the workers. The results had not been
industrially productive. The workers' committees or soviets seldom
seemed able to run the factories efficiently. The decree attempted to
recognise the legitimacy of the workers' takeover, while at the same
time asserting the need for discipline and order in the industrial
workplace:

1 In order to provide planned regulation of the national economy,
workers' control over the manufacture, purchase, sale and storage
of produce and raw materials and over the financial activity of
enterprise is introduced in all industrial, commercial, banking,
5 agricultural, co-operative and other enterprises, which employ
hired labour . . . At all enterprises the owners and the representatives of the wage and salary earners elected to exercise workers'
control are declared answerable to the state for the maintenance of
the strictest order and discipline and for the protection of
10 property.

The relative powerlessness of the Bolshevik government at this early
stage was indicated by the statistic that, for every factory formally
nationalised under the decree, four more were seized by the workforce
without government approval being sought. A Russian economist at the
time described this as 'proletarian nationalisation from below'. One of
the problems for the government was that not all the workers'
committees were dominated by Bolsheviks. Until the party gained
greater control at local and shop floor level it would be difficult for the
central government to impose its will upon the factories. Nevertheless,
the government pressed on with its plans for establishing the
framework of state direction of the economy, even if the reality of
effective central control was some way off. In December, the Supreme
Council of the National Economy (*Vesenkha*) was set up, with the
following terms of reference:

1 The Supreme Council of the National Economy will prepare
  general norms and plans for the regulation of the economic life of
  the country and co-ordinate and unify the activities of the local
  and central regulating organs (committees on fuel, metals, trans-
5 port, food supply and others) that are attached to the People's
  Commissariats (trade and industry, food, agriculture, finance,
  army and navy, etc), the All-Russian Soviet of Workers' Control,
  the factory committees, and the trade unions. The Supreme
  Council of the National Economy is to take charge of all existing
10 institutions for the regulation of economic life.

Initially, *Vesenkha* was unable to exercise the degree of authority
granted to it. However, it did preside over a number of important
developments. In 1920 a special State Commission (GOELRO) was
established to organise a nationwide system for generating electricity.
At the time, Lenin remarked that GOELRO was an example of his
belief that 'Communism equals Soviet power, plus electrification'. The
banks and the railways were nationalised, foreign debts were cancelled,
and attempts were made to bring some order to the chaotic transport
system. These were important practical achievements, which suggested
how effective centralised economic control might become should the
Bolshevik regime be able to gain real power.

2 War Communism 1918–21   *Cause - Civil War*

In the summer of 1918, Lenin abruptly abandoned state capitalism and
began to introduce a series of restrictive and rigorously-applied economic measures, which are collectively known as 'war communism'. The
chief reason for the new departure was the desperate situation created
by the Civil War. Lenin judged that the fight for survival in which the
Bolsheviks were engaged necessitated oppressive policies. The White
menace could be met only by an intensification of authority in those
regions which the Reds controlled (approximately 30 of the 50 pro-
vinces of European Russia). The change in economic strategy has to be
seen, therefore, as part of the Terror which the Bolsheviks operated in
these years (see page 118). Every aspect of life, social, political and
economic had to be subordinated to the task of winning the Civil War.

a) Industry

The first step towards war communism as a formal policy was taken in
June 1918. However, even before that date, the instruments by which it
would be imposed had already come into being. The existence of the
Cheka and the Red Army enabled Lenin to embark on a policy of
centralisation, sure in the knowledge that the means of enforcing
conformity were to hand. By that time also, there had been a

considerable increase in Bolshevik influence in the factories, achieved by the infiltration of the workers' committees by political commissars. This development helped prepare the way for the issuing of the Decree on Nationalisation in June 1918, which within two years brought practically all the major industrial enterprises in Russia under central government control. However, it was one thing to end private ownership, quite another to make the factories more productive. The workforce remained the same and, as Lenin had pointed out, industry was still dependent on the incumbent managers and specialists. Moreover, nationalisation of itself did nothing to increase industrial production. It was imposed at a time of severe industrial disruption, which had been caused initially by the strains of the war of 1914–17 but which worsened during the Civil War. Military needs were given priority, thus denying resources to those industries not considered essential. Even where supplies were available, the dislocated transport system prevented their effective distribution.

The situation was made more serious by the factories' being deprived of adequate manpower. This was a result both of conscription into the Red Army and of the flight from the urban areas of large numbers of inhabitants, who left either in search of food or to escape the Civil War. The populations of Petrograd and Moscow dropped by a half between 1918 and 1921. The problems for industry were deepened by hyperinflation. The scarcity of goods and the government's policy of continuing to print currency notes effectively destroyed the value of money. By the end of 1920, the rouble had fallen to one per cent of its worth in 1917. In 1921, train and tram fares were nominally one million times higher than in 1917. Such figures quickly became meaningless and money ceased to be a medium of exchange. Proper commercial transactions were impossible to conduct in such an atmosphere. Bartering was adopted as a substitute, but while the exchange of goods worked reasonably successfully on a small scale at local level, it could not be adapted effectively to large-scale enterprise. These factors meant that although war communism tightened the Bolshevik grip on industry it did not lead to economic growth. The table below shows the failure of war communism in economic terms.

	1913	1921
Index of gross industrial output	100	31
Index of large-scale industrial output	100	21
Coal (million tons)	29	8.9
Oil (million tons)	9.2	3.8
Electricity (million Kwhs)	2039	520
Pig iron (million tons)	4.2	0.1
Steel (million tons)	4.3	0.18
Bricks (millions)	2.1	0.01

Processed sugar (million tons)	1.3	0.05
Rail freight carried (million tons)	132.4	39.4
Imports at 1913 rouble value (millions)	1374	208
Exports at 1913 rouble value (millions)	1520	20

b) Agriculture

For Lenin, the most pressing reason for introducing war communism was the critical food shortage. The tightening of government control over agriculture was primarily intended to force the peasants to provide more food. This was not seen simply as a matter of increased food production. There was a common belief among the Bolsheviks that the richer peasants (the *kulaks*) were hoarding their grain stocks in order to keep prices artificially high. The attitude of the peasants was that it was not to their advantage to send their produce to the towns until the government, which had become the main food purchaser, was willing to pay a fair price for it. The government interpreted this as counter-revolutionary defiance and prepared to use coercion. In June 1918, the government empowered a specially-created People's Commission of Supply (*Narkomprod*) to organise committees of 'poor peasants' responsible for the collection and transporting of grain. *Narkomprod* had little success. The peasants proved more difficult to coerce than the factory workers. As a naturally conservative class, they were deeply suspicious of central government, whether tsarist or Bolshevik. Since their emancipation in 1861, even the poorest peasants had developed a strong proprietorial sense. They proved highly resistant to Bolshevik proposals for the replacement of individual land holdings with collective (*kolkhoz*) or state (*sovkhoz*) farms.

Lenin's next move was to try to overcome resistance by playing off the 'poor peasants', the 'middle peasants' and the *kulaks* against each other. However, these categories were largely Bolshevik constructs, which seldom matched the ill-defined group differences in the countryside. The assumed rivalries generally did not exist. Once this was realised, Lenin's government turned to a policy of direct coercion. *Cheka* detachments were sent into the countryside to requisition grain by force. In August 1918, the people's commissar for food issued the following orders:

1 All Soviets of Workers' and Peasants' Deputies, all committees of the poor, all trade union organisations of workers, together with the local organs of the Peoples' Commissariats of Food and Agriculture are to form immediately harvesting and grain requisi-
5 tion detachments.

The tasks of the above-mentioned detachments are to: harvest winter grain in former landlord-owned estates; harvest grain on the land of notorious *kulaks*; every food requisition detachment is

to consist of not less than 75 men and two or three machine guns.
10   The political commissar's duties are to ensure that the detachment carries out its duties and is full of revolutionary enthusiasm
and discipline.

What the orders amounted to was an official sanctioning of violence.
Between 1918 and 1921, the requisition squads systematically terro-
rised the countryside, yet the result was directly contrary to the
objective. Even less food became available. Knowing that any surplus
would simply be confiscated, the peasant resorted to subsistence
farming, producing only the barest minimum to feed himself and his
family. Nevertheless, throughout the period of war communism, the
Bolsheviks persisted in their belief that the problem was caused by the
peasants hoarding their grain. Official reports continued to speak of
'concealment, concealment everywhere, in the hopes of selling grain to
town speculators at fabulous prices'.

By 1921, the drastic fall in food production, caused by a combination
of requisitioning, drought and the general disruption of war, had
created a national famine. The grain harvests in 1920 and 1921
produced less than half that gathered in 1913. Even *Pravda* admitted in
1921 that one in five of the population was starving. Matters became so
desperate that the Bolsheviks, while careful to blame the *kulaks* and the
Whites for the situation, were prepared to admit there was a famine and
to accept foreign assistance. A number of countries supplied Soviet
Russia with aid. The outstanding contribution came from the USA in
the form of the American Relief Association (ARA). Notwithstanding
such efforts, organised relief came too late to prevent mass starvation. It
is estimated that of the ten million fatalities of the Civil War period,
over half were the result of hunger or malnutrition.

By 1921, the grim reality of the economic situation had begun to
undermine the original justification for introducing war communism.
During the period of its operation, industrial and agricultural production had fallen alarmingly. This did not mean that war communism
necessarily became unpopular among the Bolsheviks themselves. Indeed, there were many in the party who, far from regarding it as a
temporary measure introduced to meet an extreme situation, believed
that it represented true revolutionary Bolshevism. The leading economic theorists in the party, Bukharin and Preobrazhensky, who were
referred to as 'Left Bolsheviks' because of the hard-line nature of their
views, urged that war communism should be retained as the permanent
economic strategy of the Bolshevik government. They saw the centralising of industry, the ending of private ownership, and the squeezing
of the peasants as the correct application of the socialist principles of the
proletarian revolution.

Lenin himself clung to the policy as long as he could. As late as
December 1920, he was still urging that grain requisitioning should be

continued 'with strict conformity to the decree of the Soviet regime'. However, he was nothing if not a realist. The failure of the economy to recover and the scale of the famine led him to consider possible alternatives to war communism. He was finally convinced of the necessity for change by widespread anti-Bolshevik risings in 1920–1. These were a direct reaction against the rigours of the government's policy. Lenin described these risings as illuminating the true situation like a lightning flash. He responded by introducing the New Economic Policy (NEP) at the Tenth Party Congress in March 1921.

3 The New Economic Policy (NEP)

As with the policy it replaced, the NEP was intended by Lenin primarily to meet Russia's urgent need for food. Whatever the purity of the revolutionary theory behind war communism, it had clearly failed on a practical level. Coercion had proved to be an ineffective method of inducing the peasants to produce and distribute greater amounts of grain. Lenin judged, therefore, that if the peasants could not be forced they must be persuaded. He told the delegates at the Party Congress:

1 We must try to satisfy the demands of the peasants who are dissatisfied, discontented, and cannot be otherwise. In essence the small farmer can be satisfied with two things. First of all, there must be a certain amount of freedom for the small private
5 proprietor; and, secondly, commodities and products must be provided.

Disagreements within the Bolshevik Party over the NEP would emerge later, but in the spring of 1921 the severity of the famine and the depressed economic situation in Russia led the delegates to give unanimous support to Lenin's proposals. The decree declaring the NEP to be official government policy was published in *Pravda* in March 1921. It became the basis for all subsequent developments of the NEP. Its essential features were the abandonment of state requisitioning and the re-introduction of the market economy, which allowed the peasants to trade for private profit.

1 In order to assure an efficient and untroubled economic life on the basis of a freer use by the farmer of the products of his labour and of his economic resources, requisitioning, as a means of state collection of food supplies, raw material and fodder, is to be
5 replaced by a tax in kind . . .
All the reserves of food, raw material and fodder which remain with the peasants after tax has been paid are at their full disposition . . .
Exchange is permitted within the limits of local economic

10 turnover, both through co-operative organisation and through markets.

Lenin was aware that the new policy marked a retreat from the principle of state control of the economy. It re-introduced the idea of a mixed economy in which certain features of capitalism existed alongside socialism. Conscious of the unease of many Bolsheviks over this, Lenin was at pains to stress to his colleagues that the NEP was only a partial and temporary concession to capitalism. He emphasised that the party retained control of 'the commanding heights of the economy', by which he meant large-scale industry, banking and the regulation of foreign trade. He added that he was prepared 'to let the peasants have their little bit of capitalism as long as we keep the power'. To those Bolsheviks who began to question the wisdom of making concessions to the peasantry, he delivered a somewhat contradictory statement that suggests the difficulty he was experiencing in trying to justify his change of policy:

1 We retreat on this one condition alone when we introduce our New Economic Policy, so as to begin a most determined offensive after the retreat . . . We were forced to resort to 'war communism' by war and ruin. It was a temporary measure. We are still in such
5 a state of ruin that we cannot give the peasant manufactured goods for all we require. Hence, it is necessary, to a certain extent, to help to restore small industry. The effect will be the revival of the petty bourgeoisie and of capitalism. This is beyond doubt. We all agree that concessions are necessary. The proleta-
10 rian regime is in no danger as long as the proletariat firmly holds power in its hands, as long as it firmly holds transport and large-scale industry in its hands. We must not be afraid of Communists 'learning' from bourgeois specialists, and capitalists.

Lenin recognised that state requisitioning had not been the only disincentive discouraging the peasants from producing a food surplus. The disruption of industry had dried up the supply of manufactured goods, so denying the peasants the chance of buying consumer items even when they could afford them. It was vital, therefore, that agriculture should not be seen in isolation. Lenin regarded the measures relating to industrial reorganisation as important as those dealing with the land. By 1921, the centralised, bureaucratic methods of *Vesenkha* had not achieved the hoped-for advances in industry. Costs were high, but production was low. In an effort to reverse this, the NEP permitted a large degree of autonomy to small-scale industrial enterprises. The State Bank was instructed to advance loans and credit facilities. This was an aspect of the attempt to restore money to its traditional place in the economy as the principal medium of exchange, a policy consolidated in 1922 by the introduction of a newly-valued rouble.

These features of the NEP were evidence of the inability of the Bolshevik government since 1917 to restructure the Russian economy along purely ideological lines. Lenin admitted as much. He declared, in an address to the party in October 1921, that 'Our New Economic Policy means that in applying our former methods we suffered defeat and had to begin a strategic retreat'. He went on to explain why that defeat had occurred:

1 Our conception was wrong. We hoped through the decrees of the proletarian government to found state industries and organise the distribution of state products upon a Communist basis in a country that was *petit bourgeois*! Life has shown that we made a
5 mistake. A succession of transition periods such as State Capitalism and Socialism was required to prepare, through many years of preliminary work, the transition to Communism.

Lenin's argument was that it made no sense for Bolsheviks to pretend that they could pursue an economic policy which took no account of the circumstances. Foreign affairs also played a part in Lenin's thinking. By 1921, it was clear that the international proletarian revolution which he had previously envisaged was not going to take place. Therefore, at least for the present, the Russian Bolsheviks would have to concentrate on consolidating and preserving the world's only revolutionary state by whatever means available. The NEP was such a means.

Lenin's realism demanded that political theory take second place to economic necessity. It was this that troubled the members of the party, such as Trotsky and Preobrazhensky, who had regarded the repressive measures of war communism as the proper revolutionary strategy for the Bolshevik Party to follow. They were disturbed by the concessions to the peasantry and the re-emergence of capitalism that the NEP entailed. Trotsky described its introduction as 'the first sign of the degeneration of Bolshevism'. A rumour spread that the initials NEP really stood for 'New Exploitation of the Proletariat'. One of the main complaints of the objectors was that the reintroduction of money and private trading was creating a new class of 'Nepmen', a scornful term applied to those who stood to gain from the capitalism permitted under the new policy: the *kulaks*, the retailers, the traders, and the small manufacturers. It was the profiteering 'Nepmen' whom Victor Serge, a representative of the Left Bolsheviks, had in mind when he described the immediate social effects of NEP: 'the cities we ruled over assumed a foreign aspect; we felt ourselves sinking into the mire. Money lubricated and befouled the entire machine just as under capitalism'.

The argument concerning the NEP was such a divisive one that the Bolsheviks might well have split over it, had it not been for Lenin's great moral authority within the party and his ability to command personal loyalty. There was also a number of other factors that helped him to prevent division. One was that the Tenth Party Congress in 1921, at which the NEP had been formally announced, had also voted overwhelmingly in favour of Lenin's resolution 'On Party Unity'. The key passage read:

1 The Congress orders the immediate dissolution, without exception, of all groups that have been formed on the basis of some platform or other, and instructs all organisations to be very strict in ensuring that no manifestations of factionalism of any sort be
5 tolerated. Failure to comply with this resolution of the Congress is to entail unconditional and immediate expulsion from the party.

The object of this proposal was to prevent groups or 'factions' within the party from criticising government or Central Committee decisions. An accompanying resolution condemned the activities of the 'Workers Opposition', the group, largely composed of trade unionists, who had opposed the excesses of war communism and who had been involved in the Kronstadt Rising. Between them, the two resolutions on party loyalty provided a highly effective means of stifling criticism of the NEP.

At the same time as Lenin presented these strictures on party factionalism, he also declared that all political parties other than the Bolsheviks were now outlawed in the USSR. 'Marxism teaches that only the Communist Party is capable of training and organising a vanguard of the proletariat and the whole mass of the working people.' This was the logical climax of the policy, begun in 1918, of suppressing all forms of public opposition to the authority of the Bolsheviks. The value to Lenin of his announcement at this critical juncture was that it answered the charge that the NEP marked a weakening of political resolve. His declaration that Soviet Russia was now formally a one-party state strengthened his claim that the NEP was a purely economic measure, which involved no weakening of revolutionary principle. This tightening of Bolshevik authoritarianism made it extremely difficult for disgruntled Bolsheviks to assert openly that the NEP in any way jeopardised the supremacy of the party.

Another factor maintaining Bolshevik cohesion over the NEP was that Bukharin, the outstanding Left Bolshevik economist and a member of the Politburo, quickly abandoned his initial opposition to the new policy and became its most enthusiastic supporter. In 1923 he wrote that the traumatic events of 1921 had opened his eyes to the true situation. Bukharin's new approach was expressed in his appeal to the peasants: 'Enrich yourselves under the NEP'. Bukharin believed that the increased purchasing power of the peasants, which would result from the sale of their surplus grain, would stimulate productive industry. It is significant that during the final two years of Lenin's life, when he became increasingly incapacitated by a series of crippling strokes before dying in January 1924, it was Bukharin who was his closest *confidant*. The last two articles published under Lenin's name, *On Co-operation* and *Better Fewer, But Better*, were justifications of the NEP. Both were essentially the work of Bukharin.

In the event, the most powerful reason for the party to accept the NEP proved to be a statistical one. The production figures suggested that the policy worked. By the time of Lenin's death, the Soviet economy had begun to make a marked recovery under the NEP. The table below indicates the scale of the growth in agricultural and industrial output and in wages. It should be noted that Russian economic statistics, for both the tsarist and the post-1917 periods, need to be regarded with caution. The reliability of the data is suspect, either because of the unscientific way in which they were originally measured or because they were deliberately distorted for political ends. Most western analysts, such as the leading authority on Russian economic history, Alec Nove (whose table is used below), allow for this by recomputating the figures they take from Russian sources.

	1921	*1922*	*1923*	*1924*	*1925*
Agriculture					
Sown area (million hectares)	90.3	77.7	91.7	98.1	104.3
Grain harvest (million tons)	37.6	50.3	56.6	51.4	72.5
Industry					
Coal (million tons)	8.9	9.5	13.7	16.1	18.1
Steel (thousand tons)	183	39	709	1140	2135
Finished cloth (million metres)	105	349	691	963	1688
Value of factory output (million roubles)	2004	2619	4005	4660	7739
Electricity (million Kwhs)	520	775	1146	1562	2925
Rail freight carried (million tons)	39.4	39.9	58.0	67.5	83.4
Average monthly wage of urban worker (in roubles)	10.2	12.2	15.9	20.8	25.2

Lenin's claim that under the NEP the Bolsheviks would still control 'the commanding heights of the economy' was shown to be substantially correct by the census of 1923. The figures indicated that, in broad terms, the NEP had produced an economic balance; while agriculture and trade were largely in private hands, the state dominated Russian industry.

Share of Trade

Private traders ('Nepmen')	75%
The state	15%
Co-operatives	10%

	Distribution of industrial workforce	Average number of workers in each factory
Private enterprises	12%	2
State enterprises	85%	155
Co-operatives	3%	15

Impressive though the figures of recovery are, it should not be thought that the NEP was a total economic success. Its opponents could legitimately criticise it on the grounds that the balance it appeared to have achieved was notional rather than real. The fact was that industry failed to grow at the same rate as agriculture. The 'Nepmen' may have done well, but there was high unemployment in the urban areas. The disparity between agricultural and industrial growth rates led in 1923 to a situation that became known as the 'Scissors Crisis'. This was the figurative way in which Trotsky, at the Twelfth Party Congress in that year, likened the economic problem created by the widening gap between industrial and agricultural prices to the open blades of a pair of scissors.

Ironically, the crisis was caused in part by the revival of agriculture and the ending of the famine. In 1922 and 1923, kinder weather and an increase in the amount of land under cultivation produced greater harvest yields, which led naturally to a fall in the price of food. However, this was not matched by a comparable drop in the price of industrial goods. Factories took much longer than the land to recover from the damage and disruption of the Civil War, with the result that they were unable to meet the growing demand for manufactured goods. The consequent scarcity of factory products drove up their price at the same time as the increased amount of food available was reducing the cost of agricultural products. The net effect was that the peasants found that they were having to sell their produce at too low a price for them to be able to afford the inflated cost of manufactured goods. This resurrected the very problem that had prompted Lenin to adopt the NEP – the danger that the peasants would lose their incentive to produce surplus food. Should this recur, the Russian economy overall would return to the depressed condition of the war communism period.

With Lenin's illness preventing him from any longer playing an effective political role, divisions within the party re-emerged. Trotsky declined to serve on a special 'Scissors Committee' set up by the Central Committee at the height of the crisis in October 1923. Instead, he

Index of prices – 100 in 1913

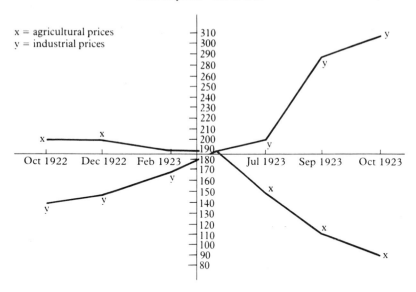

The 'Scissors Crisis'

became the spokesman of 'the Platform of 46', a group of 46 party members which issued an open public letter critical of the government's lack of an 'economic plan' and condemning the 'flagrant radical errors of economic policy' which had subordinated Soviet Russia's proletarian industrial needs to the interests of the 'Nepmen' and the petit-bourgeoisie. Trotsky's arguments were strengthened by the undeniable failure of *Vesenkha* (renamed *Gosplan* in 1921) to formulate an integrated national economic strategy. *Gosplan* issued a number of impressive-sounding pronouncements, but it achieved little in the practical field. After three years its chairman had to admit that Soviet Russia still lacked 'a single economic plan'.

The threat of confrontation between supporters and opponents of the NEP was averted, though only temporarily, by an upturn in the economy. After October 1923 the retail price of industrial goods began to fall from the critically high level of that month. Industry continued to grow and an abundant harvest guaranteed the maintenance of adequate food supplies. The blades of the scissors began to close. By 1924, industry had largely recovered from the depression into which it had sunk before the introduction of the NEP in 1921.

However, these were temporary gains; they were no guarantee of permanent economic or political stability. How long the NEP would

continue to operate and whether it genuinely represented the aspira-
tions of the Communist Party and the Soviet state were questions that
remained unsettled at the time of Lenin's death in 1924. The period
from 1917 to 1924 had shown the wide gap between revolutionary
theory and economic reality. It could be argued that Bolshevik policy in
these years, far from being a matter of structured economic planning,
was never anything more than a set of fragmented responses to a series
of desperate situations.

Making notes on 'The Bolsheviks and the Economy 1918–24'

In compiling your notes, concentrate on gaining an understanding of
the major economic developments in the period by following the
pattern of analysis that appears in the chapter. In Russian history there
has always been a very considerable overlap between political and
economic developments. This is particularly true of the period 1917–
24, so you would be well advised to make frequent cross-references to
chapter 7.

The following list of headings will assist you in ordering your
thoughts.

1.   State Capitalism 1917–18
1.1. Lenin's ideas on the transition from capitalism to socialism
1.2. The economic problems confronting the Bolshevik government
1.3. The Decree on Land
1.4. The Decree on Workers' Control
1.5. What was the role of *Vesenkha*?
2.   War Communism 1918–21
2.1. Why was war communism adopted?
2.2. Its impact upon industry
2.3. Its impact upon agriculture
2.4. Grain requisitioning
2.5. The famine
3.   The NEP 1921–4
3.1. The reasons for its introduction
3.2. What were its main features?
3.3. How did Lenin justify the NEP to the Bolshevik Party?
3.4. Lenin's attack upon factionalism
3.5. The divisions among the Bolsheviks over the NEP
3.6. The 'Scissors Crisis'
3.7. How successful was the NEP as an economic policy?

Source-based questions on 'The Bolsheviks and the Economy 1918–24'

1 State Capitalism

Study the extracts from Lenin's writings on page 128, from the Decree on Land on page 129, and from the Decree on Workers' Control on page 130. Then answer the following questions:

a) In what ways does the passage on page 128 illustrate Lenin's definition of state capitalism as a 'compromise measure'? (5 marks)
b) From your own knowledge, suggest what type of argument Lenin was trying to overcome in this passage. (6 marks)
c) How far does the evidence in the extracts from the Decrees on Land and on Workers' Control suggest that these two measures were largely concerned with authorising what had already occurred? (7 marks)
d) What impression can be gained from these three sources of the economic problems confronting the Bolsheviks in the first year after the October Revolution? (7 marks)

2 War Communism

Study the data on page 132, the requisition order on page 133, and then answer the following questions:

a) Using your own knowledge, suggest reasons for the disparity between the indices of industrial output for 1913 and 1921. (5 marks)
b) Explain the meaning of the term 'notorious kulaks' as used in the extract on page 133, line 8. (2 marks)
c) In the light of the evidence in the requisition order on page 133, comment on the judgment that the methods of collecting grain amounted to 'an official policy of violence'. (7 marks)
d) Of what value are these two sources to the historian studying the nature of war communism? (9 marks)

3 The NEP

Study the decree on page 135, Lenin's justification on page 136, and the tables on pages 139 and 140. Answer the following questions:

a) Using your own knowledge and the evidence in the decree on page 135, examine Lenin's reasons for introducing the NEP in 1921. (4 marks)
b) According to the comments in the extract on page 136, why was Lenin willing to see the revival of 'the petty bourgeoisie and of capitalism'? (4 marks)
c) Examine the strengths and limitations of the table on page 139 as evidence of the impact of the NEP on the Soviet economy. (7 marks)

d) How far does the table on page 140, showing the distribution of trade and industry, suggest that the NEP had produced an economic balance? (6 marks)

e) Using all these sources and your own knowledge, trace the development of the NEP between 1921 and 1924. (9 marks)

CHAPTER 9

Conclusion

1 The Continuity of Russian History 1881–1924

In 1881 reformers and revolutionaries were in agreement that Russia had to be modernised. Where they differed was in their view of how this was to be achieved. On occasion, tsardom dallied with the idea of reform but in the long term it showed itself unwilling to make the political adjustments comparable with the social and economic changes that were occurring. Whether tsardom would have survived but for the onset of war in 1914 must remain an open question, but the fact was that the war revealed both the fragility of the economic advance that had been achieved since the 1890s and the administrative weakness of the tsarist state. The war also showed up the emptiness of the myth of the tsar as providential protector of the Russian people. The incapacity of Nicholas II in the face of the military and political crises that confronted Russia after 1914 eroded the loyalty of the Russian people. By February 1917, no one, not even the tsar's traditional supporters, was prepared to save him. It was not the demonstrators in Petrograd, but the army high command and the aristocratic members of the duma who advised him to abdicate.

The collapse of tsardom left a power vacuum which the Provisional Government proved unable to fill. The reconstituted duma which succeeded the tsar in February held office, but it never held power. It lacked the ruthlessness which the desperate situation demanded. From the first, its authority was circumscribed by the existence of the Petrograd soviet. Unable to prosecute the war successfully and unwilling to introduce the social reforms that might have given it a popular base, the Provisional Government tottered towards collapse. When it was challenged in October by the Bolsheviks, who themselves had been on the point of political extinction in July, it was friendless. It gave in with scarcely a show of resistance. In name, it was the soviets which then took power, but in reality it was the Bolsheviks, who proceeded to turn Russia into a one-party-state. It took them three years of bitter civil war to do it, but they alone of all the political parties in post-revolutionary Russia had the necessary dedication and willingness to destroy whatever stood in their way.

All the signs were that if Russia was to be modernised it could not be done by moderate means. The brief liberal experiment that followed the February Revolution was a temporary break in the authoritarian tradition. The Provisional Government had neither the time nor the ability to lay down democratic roots. It is arguable that the authoritarian tradition was so ingrained in Russia that modernisation had to be imposed from the top. Although Lenin rejected the Russian past, he remained very much its heir. He had as little time for democracy as the tsars. Despite the upheavals of 1917, the rule of the Bolsheviks marked a continuation of absolutism in Russia. The Civil War and the foreign interventions, by intensifying the threat to the Bolshevik government, provided it with the pretext for demanding absolute conformity from the masses and the party members as the price of the Revolution's survival. Yet it is doubtful whether, even without that threat, Bolshevism could have developed other than as an oppressive system. Its dogmatic Marxist creed and its belief that it alone represented the force of history made it as intolerant of other political ideas as tsardom had been. The forcible dissolution of the Constituent Assembly in 1918 and the crushing of the Kronstadt revolt in 1921 were the clear proof that democracy would never be allowed to restrict Bolshevik control. 1917 did not mark a complete break with the past. Rather it was the replacement of one form of state authoritarianism with another.

2 Lenin's Role as a Revolutionary

Lenin proclaimed the October Revolution to be the proletarian triumph that Marx had foretold, but it is difficult to see the Bolshevik seizure of power as the victory of the Russian workers. Lenin's greatest single achievement as a revolutionary was to reshape Marxist theory to make it fit Russian conditions. The instrument with which he chose to accomplish this was the Bolshevik Party. Although Lenin was careful always to describe his policies as democratic, for him the term had a particular meaning. Democracy was not to be reckoned as a matter of numbers but as a method of Party rule. Because the party was the vehicle of historical change, its role was not primarily to win large-scale backing, but to direct the Revolution from above, regardless of the scale of popular support. 'No revolution', Lenin wrote, 'ever waits for formal majorities'. This apparent political arrogance followed logically from Lenin's view of the contemporary Russian working class. Its small size and lack of political sophistication meant that it could not achieve revolution unaided. It was, therefore, the historical mission of the enlightened Bolshevik Party to use its understanding of the scientific principles governing human society, first propounded by Marx, to guide the proletariat towards its revolutionary destiny. According to this perspective, authority emanated from the centre outwards: it was the role of the leaders to lead, the role of the party members to follow. The special term describing this was 'democratic centralism'. Lenin defined it in these terms:

1 Classes are led by parties, and parties are led by individuals who are called leaders. This is the ABC. The will of a class is sometimes fulfilled by a dictator. Soviet socialist democracy is not

in the least incompatible with individual rule and dictatorship.
5 What is necessary is individual rule, the recognition of the
dictatorial powers of one man. All phrases about equal rights are
nonsense.

It had been his concept of the unique political character of the
Bolshevik Party that had made Lenin so determined to maintain it as an
exclusive, tightly-structured, professional organisation. It is not an
exaggeration to describe Lenin's Bolsheviks as a new breed of politi-
cian: utterly self-confident, scornful of all other parties and ideas, and
totally loyal to their leader. As Trotsky expressed it: 'The party in the
last analysis is always right, because the party is the only historical
instrument given to the proletariat to resolve its fundamental tasks'.
Their ruthlessness did not guarantee their success, but it did mean that
no other party could hope to gain or hold power unless it was able to
overcome the challenge of these dedicated revolutionaries. In the event,
none of the other parties was ever remotely in a position to do this.
   It was one of Lenin's chief characteristics that he never allowed pure
theory to dictate to him. His success as a revolutionary lay in his ability
to adjust and modify theory to fit particular circumstances. This
pragmatic approach often led him to diverge from the strict pattern of
the Marxist dialectic with its clear-cut stages of class revolution, but it
made him and his followers infinitely adaptable. In his writings and
speeches he always insisted that his ideas were wholly in accordance
with those of Marx. However, in practical terms, Lenin's role in Russia
after April 1917 was that of a skilled opportunist who, with a mixture of
shrewd political judgement and luck, outmanoeuvred a collection of
opponents who never matched him in sense of purpose and sheer
determination. This entitled him to redefine the dialectical process in
the context of 1917 Russia. He introduced the notion of 'the telescoped
revolution', which asserted that the final two stages of revolution,
bourgeois and proletarian, could be compressed into one. This would
allow the Bolsheviks to organise revolution against the Provisional
Government without having to wait for the Russian proletariat to grow
substantially in size. It would not be necessary for the Russian workers
to initiate the Revolution; it would be enough that it would be carried
out in their name by the Bolsheviks, the special instruments of
historical change and the true voice of the proletariat. This readiness to
make Marxist theory conform to practical necessity was also evident in
Lenin's introduction of the NEP in 1921, a policy that entailed the
abandonment of war communism and a reversion to capitalism.
   In his reshaping of Marxism, Lenin created two enduring political
legacies – pragmatism and a redefinition of political morality. Because
the greater good of the Revolution superseded all other considerations,
nothing was impossible or unacceptable in its cause. Lenin was one of
history's great opportunists. He was perfectly clear about what his

ultimate objectives were but he was wholly unprincipled in the methods he used to achieve them. It may be said of him that he made a principle of being unprincipled. Misrepresentation and deceit were perfectly legitimate if they furthered the cause of Revolution.

This approach was wholly consistent with his interpretation of the scientific nature of Marxism. Once the premise of the historical inevitability of the proletarian revolution had been accepted, it followed that the binding duty of revolutionaries was to work for that end by whatever means necessary. To be deterred from using those necessary means merely because they were unpleasant would be to give in to bourgeois sentimentality. Indeed, it was a Marxist tenet that traditional morality was not a set of universal principles but a repressive system of control by which the bourgeoisie maintained its authority over the workers. Socialist morality deemed that lying, deception and violence were not intrinsically wrong. The question was whether their use advanced or retarded the Revolution. Put in its simplest terms, socialist morality argued that the end justified the means. Such an attitude was highly convenient in a time of struggle when the Bolsheviks were seeking to establish their authority against determined opposition. It justified the use of the most extreme methods in order to preserve the Revolution and consolidate the Bolshevik regime. 'The Terror' enforced by Lenin during the Civil War period rested upon this particular concept of conditional morality. In an address to the Congress of Komsomol (Young Communists) in 1920 Lenin remarked:

1 We say that our morality is entirely subordinated to the interests of the proletariat's class struggle. Morality is what serves to destroy the old exploiting society and to unite all the working people around the proletariat, which is building a new, a com-
5 munist society. To a communist all morality lies in this united discipline and conscious mass struggle against the exploiters. We do not believe in an eternal morality.

The belief of Lenin and the Bolsheviks that they were the special agents of historical change led logically to their claim to be superior to all other political parties. Since history was on their side, the Bolsheviks had every right to exercise control. The desperate situation in which they found themselves after the 1917 Revolution and during the Civil War period turned this theoretical into a practical necessity. Authoritarianism became an indispensable part of Communist government. Initially, there were protests from within the Bolshevik Party over this. Some members, who clung to the idea that under Communism Russia could be both socialist and democratic, were disturbed by Lenin's assumption that he was entitled to direct and control the lives of the ordinary people of Russia. Maxim Gorky warned:

1 Lenin is a gifted man who has all the qualities of a leader, including these essential ones: lack of morality and a merciless, lordly harshness towards the lives of the masses . . . As long as I can, I will repeat to the Russian proletariat, 'You are being led to
5 destruction, you are being used as material in an inhuman experiment; to your leaders, you are not human.'

Gorky's warning raises the question which still divides historians: whether the brutal totalitarianism of the Stalinist regime which operated from the late 1920s was the responsibility solely of Stalin, or whether it was a logical development of the system previously established under Lenin. However that question is answered, it has to be observed that the principal instruments of Stalin's tyranny were already in existence by the time of Lenin's death. The one-party state, the secret police, the ban on factionalism (which effectively prohibited criticism of government or party policy), the destruction of the trade unions as an independent force representing the workers: these totalitarian features had all come into being by 1924. It is also true that under Lenin's guidance the first steps had been taken towards institutionalising the 'purge', the system of ruthless suppression of opposition by means of public show trials. Purges were to be the outstanding feature of Stalin's terror strategy, but their mechanism was already in place by 1924. The first show trial was conducted in the USSR in 1922, when, under the measures creating the one-party state introduced by Lenin in 1921 at the Tenth Party Congress, a group of SRs were publicly tried and condemned. At the time of the trial, Lenin wrote to the commissar for justice: 'In my opinion it is necessary to extend the death penalty by shooting to all types of conspiratorial activity.'

The term 'unfinished revolution' is an appropriate description of what had happened in Russia down to 1924. For the last two years of his life, Lenin's physical frailty seriously limited his control over events. There are signs that he was angered or dismayed by many of the developments within the government and the party, but was too unwell to prevent them. His views on the leading Bolsheviks were neither complimentary nor optimistic. In a series of dictated notes, known as his 'Last Will and Testament', he was sharply critical of his colleagues: Trotsky, Stalin and Bukharin were singled out as having serious character faults or political weaknesses. However, Lenin made no provision for what should follow after his death. He intimated that some form of collective leadership might be adopted, but he gave no clear instructions as to how this was to be organised. This made a power struggle after his death unavoidable.

As an international revolutionary, Lenin had originally expected that the successful Bolshevik seizure of power in October 1917 would be the first stage in a worldwide proletarian uprising. When this proved mistaken, he had to adjust to a situation in which Bolshevik Russia became an isolated revolutionary state, beset by internal and external enemies. This involved him in another major reformulation of Marxist theory. Marx had taught that proletarian revolution would be an international class movement. Yet the 1917 Revolution had been the work not of a class but of a party and had been restricted to one nation. Lenin explained this in terms of a delayed revolution; the international rising would occur at some point in the future, but in the interim Soviet Russia must consolidate its own individual revolution. This placed the Bolshevik government and its international agency, the Comintern, in an ambiguous position. What was their essential role to be? At Lenin's death, this question – whether the USSR's primary aim was world revolution or national survival – was still unresolved.

Using the Conclusion

The conclusion offers three main arguments:

1. Despite the upheavals of war and revolution there is a strong continuity in the Russian history of this period.
2. The Bolshevik *coup* in October 1917 did not mark a real break with the past, since, although the form of government changed, its essentially authoritarian and non-representative character did not.
3. 1917 was not a victory for Marxism, since Lenin in his leadership and consolidation of the Revolution did not follow or fulfil strict Marxist theory.

It would help you to ensure that you have acquired an effective 'over-view' of the topic if you were to test the validity of these three propositions by measuring them against the notes you made on the earlier chapters of the book, and by asking yourself how far they accord with the viewpoints of the other writers whose work you have studied on this period.

Chronology

1870	birth of Vladimir Ulyanov (Lenin).
1881	assassination of Alexander II by 'The People's Will'. accession of Alexander III. League of the Three Emperors. introduction of the repressive 'temporary laws'.
1881–95	Pobedonostsev as chief minister presides over 'the Reaction'.
1885	new criminal code.
1887	University Statute restricting academic freedoms Re-insurance Treaty. execution of Lenin's elder brother.
1889	creation of land captains.
1890	*Zemstva* Act.
1891–1902	construction of the Trans-Siberian Railway.
1892	Franco-Russian Convention.
1893–1903	Sergei Witte as minister of finance introduces economic reforms associated with 'the great spurt'.
1894	accession of Nicholas II.
1897	formation of Jewish Bund.
1898	SD Party formed.
1902	Lenin's pamphlet, *What Is To Be Done*, published.
1903	SDs split into Mensheviks and Bolsheviks.
1904	Anglo-French Entente.
1904–5	Russo-Japanese War.
1905	January – Bloody Sunday massacre marks the start of the 1905 Revolution. February onwards – wave of strikes and nationwide unrest. March – Russian defeat at Mukden. May – 'Union of Unions' formed, led by Milyuk Russian fleet destroyed at Tsushima. June – mutiny aboard the battleship *Potemkin* August – consultative duma announced.

September – Russo-Japanese peace treaty signed.
fresh wave of industrial strikes.
October – Kadet Party formed.
formation of St Petersburg soviet.
St Petersburg crippled by a general strike.
tsar issues October Manifesto.
November – formation of Moscow soviet.
December – Moscow soviet suppressed by force.

1906   April – Fundamental Laws promulgated by Nicholas II.
April–June – first duma.
August – Stolypin appointed as chief minister.

1906–11   Stolypin introduces a series of agrarian reforms.

1907   February–June – second duma.
November – beginning of third duma.
Rasputin enters tsar's court.
Triple Entente between France, Russia and Britain.

1908   annexation of Bosnia-Herzegovina by Austria–Hungary.

1911   September – assassination of Stolypin.

1912   serious disturbances in Lena goldfields, Siberia.
June – end of third duma.
November – start of fourth duma.
Pravda published.

1912–13   Balkan Wars.

1914–17   First World War in which Russia undergoes military defeat and experiences growing social and political unrest.

1914   June – assassination of Franz Ferdinand at Sarajevo.
29 July – Russian full mobilisation orders given.
1 August – Germany declares war on Russia.
August – suspension of fourth duma.

1915   June–July – duma reconvened.
June – Progressive Bloc formed.
August – tsar becomes commander-in-chief.

1916   November – duma reconvened.
December – murder of Rasputin.

1917   February Revolution – 18 February–4 March.
18 February – strike begins at Putilov factories.
23 February – International Women's Day.
workers' demonstrations.
25 February – general strike.
27 February – unofficial meeting of committee of duma.

first meeting of Petrograd soviet.

28 February – Nicholas II attempts to return to Petrograd, but is prevented from doing so.

1 March – Soviet 'Order Number 1'.

2 March – Provisional Government formed from duma committee.

Nicholas signs Decree of Abdication.

3 March – new government publicly declared.

4 March – formal declaration of Romanov abdication.

14 March – soviet issues an *Address to the people of the whole world.*

3 April – Lenin returns to Petrograd.

4 April – Lenin issues *April Theses.*

26 June – major offensive launched against Austro-German armies on the south-western front.

2 July – Ukrainian issue leads to ministerial crisis.

3–6 July – July Days uprising.

6 July – Lenin flees from Petrograd.

8 July – Kerensky becomes prime minister.

18 July – Kornilov becomes commander-in-chief.

August – advance of German forces threatens Petrograd.

26 August–1 September – the Kornilov affair.

25 September – Bolsheviks gain a majority in Petrograd soviet and elect Trotsky as chairman.

7 October – Lenin slips back into Petrograd.

10 October – Bolshevik Central Committee commits itself to armed insurrection.

12 October – Petrograd soviet sets up MRC.

23 October – Kerensky orders closing down of *Pravda* and *Izvestiya.* Lenin instructs the Bolsheviks to begin the rising against Kerensky's government.

24 October – first session of the Congress of Soviets.

24–5 October – Bolsheviks take control of Petrograd.

25–6 October – Kerensky leaves Petrograd, hoping to rally support, but fails.

Bolsheviks take the Winter Palace.

26 October – Bolsheviks establish *Sovnarkom*, with Lenin as chairman.

27 October – Lenin informs the Congress of Soviets that the Bolshevik-led Petrograd soviet has seized power in their name.

8 November – Bolsheviks issue the Decrees on Land, on Peace, and on Workers' Control.

11 November – elections for Constituent Assembly begin.

1 December – *Vesenkha* established.

2 December – armistice signed at Brest-Litovsk.

	7 December – *Cheka* created.
1918–20	the Russian Civil War, Reds *v* Whites.
1918	5–6 January – meeting and dissolution of the Constituent Assembly. 15 January – decree establishing the Red Army. 3 March – Treaty of Brest-Litovsk. 12 March – Soviet capital transferred to Moscow. 4 April – beginning of foreign interventions. May – Czech Legion begins to create problems for the Bolsheviks, which marks the start of the Civil War. June – Decree on Nationalisation. July – beginning of forced grain requisitions from the peasants. 4 July – Russian state becomes RSFSR. 16–17 July – murder of tsar and family at Ekaterinburg. 5 September – Red Terror officially introduced.
1919	March – first Congress of the Comintern. Bolshevik Party renamed the Communist Party.
1920	February – GOELRO established. April – Red Army marches into Poland. November – the Civil War effectively ends with the defeat of the Whites in the Crimea.
1921	March – Kronstadt Rising. March – Lenin introduces the NEP at the 10th Conference of the CPSU, which also accepts the decree against factionalism.
1922–3	Lenin suffers a number of increasingly severe strokes that limit his ability to control events.
1922	December – Soviet state becomes the USSR. Lenin completes his 'testament', critical of all the leading Bolsheviks.
1923	October – the 'Scissors Crisis'.
1924	21 January – Lenin's death.

Glossary

Bolshevik	the name (meaning 'majority') taken by Lenin and his followers after the split in the SD Party in 1903.
bourgeoisie	the Marxist term for the exploiting capitalist middle class.
Bund	an organisation formed by revolutionary Jews.
CCCP	Central Committee of the Communist Party.
Cheka	All Russian Extraordinary Commission for Fighting Counter-Revolution (the Bolshevik secret police).
Comintern	the Communist International organisation, established in 1919 for the purpose of bringing about revolution in other countries.
commissar	minister or official in the Soviet government or CPSU.
CPSU	the Communist Party of the Soviet Union (formerly the Bolshevik Party).
Diktat	a settlement imposed by threat of force.
duma	the imperial Russian parliament between 1906 and 1917.
émigrés	those who fled Russia to avoid government oppression.
ghetto	the Jewish quarters in a town or city.
glasnost	Russian for 'openness', adopted as a description of the new Soviet approach of the late 1980s and 1990s.
GOELRO	a special state commission, established in 1920 to organise the electrification of Russia.
Gosplan	superseded *Vesenkha* in 1921 as the body responsible for integrated national economic planning.
intelligentsia	the educated and more enlightened members of Russian society, who were usually supporters of reform.
Iskra	Russian for 'the spark', an SD newspaper, founded by Lenin and Martov in 1898.
Izvestiya	Russian for 'the news', taken as the title of a Bolshevik newspaper.

Kadets (KDs)	the Constitutional Democrats, a liberal party, founded in 1905.
kolkhozy	the collective farms.
Komsomol	the Young Communist League, a movement for young people between the ages of 14 and 28.
kulaks	the class of rich peasants.
Marxism/Leninism	the official Bolshevik/Communist ideology based on the theories of Karl Marx.
Mensheviks	the word (meaning 'minority') used to describe the followers of Plekhanov after the split in the SD Party in 1903.
mir	the village commune.
MRC	the military revolutionary committee of the Petrograd soviet.
Narkomprod	the People's Commission of Supply.
Narodniks	Russian for 'the people', the Populist movement that looked to the peasants to take the lead in the transforming of Russia.
NEP	the New Economic Policy, introduced by Lenin in 1921.
Nepmen	the class of merchants and middlemen who profited from the NEP.
Octobrists	the moderate reformist party, established in 1905.
Okhrana	the tsarist secret police.
Orgburo	the CCCP's bureau of organisation.
pogroms	state-organised persecutions of the Jews.
Politburo	the Political Bureau, the inner cabinet of the CCCP.
Pravda	Russian for 'truth', taken as the title of a Bolshevik newspaper which was established in 1912.
proletariat	the Marxist term for the revolutionary working class.
RSFSR	the Russian Socialist Federal Soviet Republic, the title of the Soviet state between 1918 and 1922.
SDs	the Social-Democratic Workers' Party which divided into Bolshevik and Menshevik wings in 1903.
sovkhozy	the state farms.
Sovnarkom	the Council of People's Commissars (the government of the USSR).
SRs	the Social Revolutionary Party, which developed out of the Populist movement.

Trudoviks	the labour group on the moderate wing of the SRs.
USSR	the Union of Soviet Socialist Republics, which replaced the RSFSR as the official title of the Soviet state after 1922.
verst	a unit of measurement (two-thirds of a mile).
Vesenkha	the Supreme Council of the National Economy.
Vyperod	Russian for 'forward', adopted by Lenin as the title of a Bolshevik journal.
Zemgor	the union of municipal councils and *zemstva* that combined in 1914 to further the Russian war effort.
zemstva	local government councils in the countryside, established in 1864.

Acknowledgements

The Publishers would like to thank the following for permission to reproduce material in this volume:
Extract from Alec Nove *An Economic History of the USSR* (Penguin Books, Revised edition, 1976 and © Alec Nove, 1969, 1976) reproduced by kind permission of Penguin Books Ltd.

Every effort has been made to trace and acknowledge ownership of copyright. The Publishers will be glad to make suitable arrangements with any copyright holders whom it has not been possible to contact.

The Publishers would also like to thank the following for their permission to reproduce copyright illustrations:
The Hulton Picture Company page 95; The Mansell Collection page 84; Novosti Picture Library cover, pages 11, 89; Ullstein Bilderdienst page 68.

Further Reading

1 Outline Surveys

Students are advised to broaden their understanding of the wider period before specialising further in particular topics. A book which is especially helpful as an introduction is:

J. N. Westwood, *Endurance and Endeavour: Russian History, 1812–1980* (OUP, 1973)

A book of similar value is:

L. Kochan, *The Making of Modern Russia* (Penguin, 1977)
Like Westwood's book (though much shorter), it covers an extended period and makes an excellent introduction to a broad sweep of modern Russian history.

2 Advanced Textbooks

Arguably, the leading contemporary authority on modern Russian history is **Richard Pipes**. His two major works, which between them cover the period, are:

Russia Under the Old Regime (Penguin, 1987)
The Russian Revolution 1899–1919 (Collins Harvill, 1990)

These are long books, but, since they represent the most up-to-date research on all the important topics of the period down to the establishment of Bolshevik rule, they are of particular value. They also contain excellent bibliographies. Students are encouraged to compare Pipes' books with the outstanding study from an older generation:

E. H. Carr, *The Bolshevik Revolution, 1917–23* (first published by Macmillan in 1950 as part of a multi-volume history of Soviet Russia).

Despite its title, the work analyses the period from 1898 onwards. There is a also a convenient single volume, whose earlier chapters are relevant to the period:

E. H. Carr, *The Russian Revolution from Lenin to Stalin, 1917–29* (Macmillan, 1979)

3 Biographies

Lenin remains the dominant figure of the period. Of the many books which analyse his career and achievements, three are recommended as offering students an insight into the controversy that continues to surround him. A short, critical, but very lively study is:

G. Katkov and H. Shukman, *Lenin's Path to Power* (Macdonald, 1971)

A sympathetic view of Lenin is given in:

T. Cliff, *Lenin* (Bookmarks, 1987)

This should be compared with the hostile treatment of Lenin contained in a biography by one of his SD contemporaries:

David Shub, *Lenin* (Penguin, 1966)

Despite having been treated in Stalin's Russia as a 'non-person', Trotsky is now widely recognised as having been the organiser of the October Revolution. A very long, but very readable biography is:

Isaac Deutscher, *Trotsky* (OUP, 3 volumes, 1954–70)

4 Specialist Studies

Students need to appreciate the great importance of economics in the development of Russia in this period. The most accessible study, which begins with an analysis of the economy of imperial Russia, remains:

Alec Nove, *An Economic History of the USSR* (Penguin, 1976)

One of the most readable accounts of the the collapse of the Romanovs is still:

Hugh Seton Watson, *The Decline of Imperial Russia* (Methuen, 1952)

Students wishing to understand the details of imperial Russia's war effort are likely to be stimulated by the treatment of the theme by an outstanding, if controversial, modern historian:

Norman Stone, *The Eastern Front* (Hodder and Stoughton, 1975)

The struggle of the Bolsheviks to survive after 1917 is well covered by a book which is much more than a military history:

E. Mawdsley, *The Russian Civil War* (Allen and Unwin, 1987)

Index